THE IMPACT OF 'TORONTO'

The Impact of 'Toronto'

Reports from *Renewal* magazine

edited by
WALLACE BOULTON

MONARCH
Crowborough

British Library Cataloguing Data
A catalogue record for this book is available
from the British Library.

ISBN 1 85424 315 2

Produced by Bookprint Creative Services
P.O. Box 827, BN21 3YJ, England for
MONARCH PUBLICATIONS
Broadway House, The Broadway
Crowborough, E. Sussex, TN6 1HQ
Printed in Great Britain.

Contents

Contributors

The Rev Dr Michael Green was formerly professor of evangelism at Regent College, Vancouver, and is a popular author. He is adviser in evangelism to the Archbishops of Canterbury and York and joint co-ordinator of the Springboard initiative for the Decade of Evangelism.

Eleanor Mumford worked in the Anglican church for eight years with her husband John before they joined the staff of the Anaheim Vineyard in 1985. They returned to England in 1987 to plant the South-West London Vineyard, where Eleanor is an assistant pastor.

Terry Virgo, leader of New Frontiers, is completing two years in Columbia, Missouri, working with the Christian Fellowship of Columbia, after which he expects to return to the Church of Christ the King in Brighton.

The Rev Dr Graham Twelftree is minister of Hope Valley Uniting Church in South Australia. He is a frequent contributor to commentaries in both the UK and the US, including *A Dictionary of Jesus and the Gospels* (IVP).

Peter Nodding is pastoral leader at the Millmead Centre, the Baptist church in Guildford.

John Peters teaches English language and literature at Charterhouse, Godalming, writes biographies and is on the leadership team of the King's Church, Aldershot.

The Rev Dr R T Kendall came to England from Kentucky to study at Oxford, where he gained his doctorate in 1976. A year later he succeeded Dr Martyn Lloyd-Jones as minister at Westminster Chapel.

Gerald Coates, well-known speaker and writer, leads the Pioneer team that cares for an international network of churches. He has been involved, with colleagues, in launching March for Jesus and the AIDS initiative ACET.

Helen Terry is a trained journalist and teacher. She was on the staff of *Which Computer*? magazine and is a contributor to *Woman Alive*.

The Rev Bob Redrup is vicar of Kea, Cornwall. He writes on computing for *Renewal* and, under a pseudonym, each month for a leading computer magazine.

The Rev Dr Mark Stibbe is vicar of Grenoside, Sheffield, an author, and lecturer in biblical studies at Sheffield University.

Jane Grayshon is the author of several books and is a nurse and midwife. She and her husband Matthew, a minister, and their two children are in a parish in west London.

Andy Fitz-Gibbon is Baptist minister engaged in studying social ethics at Glasgow University. **Jane** is a dental therapist. Together they shepherd a new network of home churches in Northumberland.

The Rev Dr Ron Davies is director of the post-graduate centre at All Nations Bible College, Ware, Hertfordshire, and author of *I Will Pour Out My Spirit*, a book on revivals and evangelical awakenings (Monarch).

The Rev John Leach is vicar of St James', Styvechale, Coventry. **Chris Leach** has led successful charismatic children's ministries in three churches, in Norfolk, Sheffield and now Coventry.

The Rev Nicky Gumbel was a practising barrister before entering the ordained ministry. Curate at Holy Trinity, Brompton, he is director of the Alpha course programme there, a venture which has spread to 1,000 churches.

The Rev Mike Breen became rector of St Thomas' Church, Crookes, Sheffield, after working for two years with Baptists and Anglicans in Little Rock, Arkansas.

The Rev Peter Gammons is director of Reach Out Ministries and founder and principal of Westward College, a new mission training centre at Romsey in Cambridgeshire.

The Rev Wallace Boulton, editor of *Renewal*, was head of publicity for an international group of chemical companies before being ordained. He is a former editor of the *Church of England Newspaper* and edits the Church Missionary Society magazine. He assists in the ministry at St Leonards parish church, East Sussex, and is a guild chaplain at St Bride's, Fleet Street.

Preface

The July 1994 issue of *Renewal* was at the printers when news reached us of extraordinary events unfolding at the South-west London Vineyard and other London churches, including Holy Trinity, Brompton, and St Paul's, Onslow Square. We were able to make a last-minute adjustment to get in a stop-press page headed 'Spreading like wildfire'. The 'Toronto blessing' had come to Britain and it has been a running story ever since.

I have put together this selection of articles and reports from *Renewal* on the spread of this movement of the Holy Spirit across the country, together with the comments and assessments of some of those most closely involved, and there is the added dimension of reports from Terry Virgo in the United States and Graham Twelftree in Australia. I hope that this volume will form a valuable part of the record of what the Lord has been doing in these days, in his church and in the lives of individual Christians. I believe that it makes a worthwhile and distinctive contribution to the literature which is growing up around 'Toronto' and I hope that its open and positive approach will make it a blessing and encouragement to all who read it.

God's Spirit is moving among us, with refreshing and releasing power. Momentous though this is, it is not, however, the longed-for revival which would shake and change the nation. It could be a preliminary, a preparation. We are at a critical stage. I take up this theme in the closing chapter.

I am grateful to Tony and Jane Collins for encouraging me to produce this book, and to all those who have written or been interviewed. I also thank Michael Green for allowing me to adapt, as the introduction, a paper on the 'Toronto blessing' which he prepared for some of the Church of England bishops in September 1994.

Wallace Boulton
February 1995

Introduction
by the Rev Dr Michael Green

Randy Clark, the founding pastor of the Vineyard in St Louis, was hungry for more of God and more fruitfulness in his ministry. He was powerfully touched through the ministry of a South African evangelist, Rodney Howard-Browne, and shared what had happened at the Vineyard National Board in October 1993. There was a limited outbreak of unusual phenomena there. Among those present was John Arnott, pastor of the Airport Vineyard in Toronto. He invited Clark to come to his church, which was small and unpretentious, in January 1994. Two days of meetings turned into a continuous ministry every day, except Monday evenings, to a packed church. (This has now continued for a whole year.)

The worship is very ordinary North American stuff: band, worship songs, address, and is accompanied by aircraft noise. There is no attempt at hype and the pastoral team are self-effacing and are amazed by what has happened and by the plane-loads coming in from all over the world to see what is going on.

The phenomena are mainly shaking, falling to the ground (usually backwards, and people never hurt themselves), 'drunkenness', weeping, laughing and revelations (dreams, prophetic words while under the influence). Sometimes people are unconscious for a long time, and sometimes they have no knowledge of what has been going on, or why it should have happened to them. Others realise that God has been dealing with a specific area of their own needs. The outcome seems generally to be a deep love for Jesus, and other people, coupled with a profound sense of joy.

Are these phenomena biblical? They certainly form no part of Christian theology or ethics as found in Scripture, and therefore they are in no sense normative. However, Scripture reveals a wide variety of experiences which the people of God have sometimes had under the impact of the Spirit of God. *Ruach* in the Old Testament frequently has the sense of a divine invading force, evident in biblical times when God is actively at work.

Thus *falling* before the Lord, the most notable part of this experience, is not uncommon in Scripture (Deuteronomy 9.18, Ezekiel 1.28, Daniel 8.17; 10.9, Acts 4.9, Revelation 1.17, etc). It is a reaction to the perceived presence of God (John 18.6 is an interesting parallel).

Shaking, another common phenomenon, is also to be found in Scripture, though not very often (Daniel 10.8-10, Psalms 99.1, Habakkuk 3.16, Acts 4.31). It cannot be ruled out as an appropriate response to God.

'*Drunkenness*', or being so full of the Spirit that the limbs are unco-ordinated, is also to be found in Scripture (Jeremiah 23.9 is significant, along with Acts 2.13ff and Ephesians 5.18).

Crying and laughter both constitute a release of the emotions, which have been kept very much in check by traditional church practices and by our emphasis on the intellect. Both are to be found in Scripture of course (Nehemiah 8.9, 2 Chronicles 34.27, Acts 2.37 etc, along with Psalms 126, Ecclesiastes 3.4, John 17.13). Joy and laughter fit in with the general flow of Scripture, as does weeping over one's past hurts and sins.

Revelations from God figure prominently in the Bible. That same God is not dead! See Numbers 11.29 (and note 'when the Spirit rested on them', v25), Isaiah 22.14, Jeremiah 1–11ff, 1 Samuel 10.10, Acts 2.17f (where *kai propheteuousi* is absent from Joel. The gloss shows that prophetic utterance was a notable part of the experience of the first Christians). 1 Corinthians 12-14 is of course largely concerned with revelations.

Are these phenomena unprecedented in Christian history? By no means. Here are some examples.

Jonathan Edwards writes: 'Many have had their religious affections raised far beyond what they had ever been before; there were instances of some people lying in a sort of trance, remaining for perhaps 24 hours motionless and with their senses locked up: in the meantime it was as if they went to heaven and there was a vision of glorious and delightful objects.' Or 'I had not spoken for more than a quarter of an hour when an awful solemnity seemed to settle upon them; the congregation began to fall from their seats in every direction and cried for mercy. If I had a sword in each hand I could not have cut them down so fast. Nearly the whole congregation was either on their knees or prostrate.'

John Wesley writes: 'Immediately one that stood by (to our no small surprise) cried aloud with the utmost vehemence even as in the agonies of death. But we continued in prayer until a new song was put in her mouth, a thanksgiving to our God. Soon after, two other persons were seized with strong pain, and constrained to roar for the disquietness of their hearts. These also found peace.'

George Fox writes: 'The priest scoffed at us and called us "Quakers". But the Lord's power was so over them and the word of life was declared in such authority and dread to them, that the priest himself began trembling and one of his people said "Look, the priest trembles and shakes. He is turned Quaker too."'

Jonathan Edwards on laughter and tears: 'It was very wonderful to see how persons' affections were sometimes moved when God did open their eyes to the greatness of his grace, the fullness of Christ and his readiness to save. Their joyful surprise has caused their hearts as it were to leap, so that they have been ready to break forth into laughter, tears often at the same time issuing like a flood, and intermingling loud weeping . . . The manner of God's work on the soul is very mysterious sometimes.'

It is indeed! But we would be unwise to write off these phenomena, strange though they seem.

What is the purpose of all this? It is certainly not a revival in the true sense of the word, but equally it is certainly significant, a time of refreshing from the presence of the Lord. These phenomena are a sign of God's presence among us. They are a rebuke to the this-worldliness of current Christianity. They are a rebuke to the rationalism which has dogged much of our theology for two hundred years.

They are a challenge to us to allow God to have his way with us, not to retain the control which is so dear to us. (One way of looking at 'falling' is to see it as God withdrawing our strength.) They can mark a particular work of God deep in the soul of which the recipient is cognitively unaware, but whose fruits soon become evident.

'Manifestations,' wrote John White, 'while they may be a blessing, are no guarantee of anything . . . Your fall and your shaking may be a genuine expression of the Spirit resting upon you. But the Spirit may not benefit you in the least if God does not have his way with you, while someone who neither trembles nor falls may profit greatly.'

There are biblical warnings in this area (Matthew 24.24, 2 Corinthians 11.14 and 1 John 4.1 are all significant). Key texts for proper discernment are Luke 11.9–12, 1 John 4.2,3, 1 Corinthians 12.7,10 and 14.40, Matthew 12.24–28, Galatians 5.22.

There are questions which may help discernment. Are the people genuinely praying to God? Is Jesus being exalted? Is the tone of the meeting peaceful (even if perhaps noisy?), and are the leaders self-effacing? Does love, praise and expectancy mark the congregation? Is undue importance ascribed to particular phenomena? Is the fruit good?

When people are open to this sort of spiritual experience, it is wise to have some Christians experienced in deliverance ministry available. Several of us have found demonic manifestations emerging in some people at those times: they need private and skilled ministry.

How is the blessing spreading? It would be a mistake to think that this is a contagion from Toronto. It is breaking out in many parts of the world quite spontaneously. Indeed, it is only an intensification of what is often found in spiritual ministry: I have known people 'rest in the Spirit' for many years, and it is the norm in an Anglican diocese like Sabah: when people are prayed for, they often slip to the ground. Toronto is only the occasion, not the essence – and the same is true of Holy Trinity, Brompton in this country. These phenomena are taking place in small village churches which have never heard of Toronto. It is, I think, part of the divine humour to start a large-scale movement like this out of a shop-front church that nobody had ever heard of.

What is the fruit? The Bishop of London robustly said, 'I don't mind them falling down. What I want to know is whether they are any good when they get up!' That says it all. The result seems to be that they generally *are* some good when they get up, in the following ways:

- [ ] There is a prevailing sense of joy, which tends to remain
- [ ] There is generally an intensified love for Jesus
- [ ] There is a lot of healing going on in and through this experience
- [ ] There is discernment of areas of service and empowerment for them
- [ ] There is a significant number of lapsed members returning to the church.

That is their experience in Toronto. There are some new conversions, but this does not seem to be a main part of the current move of the Spirit. It may come.

How should church leaders advise? We should neither encourage nor scoff at the particular phenomena, but we should strongly affirm anything which produces more love, more Christlikeness and more healing. Deep things can happen to people while they are prostrate. I have seen God release people into tears or laughter who were previously very uptight and had repressed hurts from their childhood. The result was a new liberation.

Any attempt to make any of these experiences normative should be resisted, but we should make it clear that God is God and cannot be contained within any of our little boxes. Any attempt at hype or showmanship must be resisted at once. We might do well to encourage those who criticise to take the attitude of Gamaliel.

There will be flotsam and jetsam on the edges of the rising tide: there always is. Wise pastoral care is imperative. Discernment is the most important requisite when any spiritual gifts are happening.

In a word, I rejoice. There are dangers, but the dangers of life are infinitely preferable to those of death.

I

'Spreading like wildfire'

'I went to Toronto because I have never been slow to go to a party,' said **Eleanor Mumford**, wife of the senior pastor of the South-west London Vineyard. 'I also went because I felt that I was spiritually bankrupt, and I went with tremendous expectancy.' She could not possibly have foreseen what would happen when she related her experiences. This is part of what she said.

I have just been on a trip to a church in Toronto. A Baptist pastor who is increasingly involved in what is going on there has written:

'There has come a notable renewal and revival of hope, faith and expectation. The Spirit of God has been pouring out freedom, joy and power. For six nights a week, between 350 and 800 people gather for worship. Over 2,000 pastors and clergy have received ministry. They think now that in the course of the last 130 days over a quarter of a million people have come to meetings at the Vineyard and Baptist churches in the area. It is far beyond any one church or denomination. With all this has come a renewing of commitment, and a rekindled passion for Jesus and the work of the Kingdom.'

The Airport Vineyard is just a very ordinary little church set in an office block, filled with ordinary people. As the worship leader strummed his guitar, he asked, 'What have you come for?' We all said, 'We've come for the Lord. We've come for more of God.' He responded, 'Well, if you've come for God you won't be disappointed.'

There was a beauty on those who were ministering there – the sort of beauty that I guess people saw in Acts when they looked at the disciples and said, 'These people have been with Jesus.' These were men and women who had spent 130 days in the company of Jesus. Like Stephen, their faces shone.

I saw the power of God poured out in incredible measure. I saw many very weary pastors who turned up with their even wearier wives, and they were so anointed by the Lord. One very sensible middle-aged man had been in pastoral ministry for years. One evening he stood up to talk about the intimacy he had gained with Jesus, and then one of the leaders prayed for him. Down he went and rolled on the floor for the next two hours. No one took any notice: he just continued to commune with God.

One pastor, a very serious young man, was not at all sure of what he had come to. For a day or two he watched and listened. Then to his embarrassment he began to shake and laugh in the presence of the Lord, and this overflowing of joy continued after his return to his own church. He had a keen sense of responsibility, however, and to keep things on the road he went into the church office to handle some paperwork. As he typed out the bulletin he came to the announcement about a forthcoming seminar entitled, 'Come Holy Spirit', and fell afresh under the power of the Lord.

God is sending us his joy and refreshing our spirits, just because he loves us. It's about his nearness to me and my dearness to him. It's contagious. One young woman left a service to get a snack. In a Mexican restaurant nearby she saw a family sitting together at a table, and completely out of character she went over to them and said, 'Would you like to be saved?' They all said yes. The whole family was led to Christ.

I went to a Christian school in Clapham the other day. I talked to the children about the Lord, and I prayed for them. The Holy Spirit fell upon those five-year-olds and they were laughing and weeping and crying out to the Lord. The teachers were affected, the parents were rolling around. I thought, 'God, this is a glorious thing you are doing. This is fantastic.'

Jesus is breaking down the barriers of his church. We have been meeting with Baptist pastors, New Frontiers pastors, Anglicans, and God is pouring his Spirit out on all of us. God is moving across London and England in a fantastic way. I cannot get over the excitement of being alive now, at this time in history.

But what are the results of all this? For myself, there is a greater love for Jesus than I have ever known, a greater excitement about the Kingdom than I ever thought possible. I have not had such an appetite for ministry for years. Jesus is restoring his joy, and his laughter is like medicine to my soul.

We have seen in the course of the last week in our church that people are getting freed and getting healed. I talked yesterday with a woman who has been mightily affected by the laughter of the Lord. She said, 'I was brought up during the last war. I always had what I needed but I never had sweets or party dresses. I never knew joy. Jesus has given me joy in the last week which has made up for all my childhood.'

The pastor at the Airport Vineyard in Toronto said, 'I didn't know God could be so much fun.' The Prodigal Son went to look for parties but he discovered that the best party was in his father's house. Isn't that the truth?

2

A mighty wind from Toronto

Churches in south-west London began to experience an astonishing outpouring of the Holy Spirit following Eleanor Mumford's return from Toronto. This account is based on the diary of events at Holy Trinity, Brompton.

The story begins far from London, at a little church near the end of the runway at Toronto Airport in Canada. In January 1994 the Holy Spirit began to fall in a new and powerful way upon members of that Vineyard church. As the extraordinary outpouring of the Holy Spirit continued, pastors from North America, and then from other parts of the world, began to travel to Toronto to see and experience for themselves what was happening.

Back home in Kingston after her visit there, Eleanor Mumford spoke briefly to several church leaders about her experience and then prayed for them to be filled with the Holy Spirit. Everyone present was affected in a remarkable way and the session continued unabated throughout lunch. Among those present were Nicky Gumbel, curate at Holy Trinity, Brompton, and his wife Pippa. Nicky Gumbel suddenly realised that he should have been back at Holy Trinity for a staff business meeting. He hurried there, to find the meeting about to break up.

He apologised and spoke briefly about what had happened.

Everyone was in a hurry to get on with other matters and Nicky Gumbel was asked to say a closing prayer. He asked the Holy Spirit to fill everyone in the room. The effect was instantaneous. The Holy Spirit touched all those present in ways few had ever experienced or seen. People fell to the ground again and again. Other people walking past the room were also affected. The news spread to those in other offices and they too were powerfully touched by the Holy Spirit. Prayer was still continuing after 5pm.

On the following Sunday, 29 May, Eleanor Mumford spoke at the morning service at Holy Trinity. At the end, she prayed for the Holy Spirit to come. There was a time of silence. Then slowly, members of the congregation began to cry quietly, and some to laugh. As the Holy Spirit came, Eleanor asked people to come forward if they wanted prayer. Many did so. As Eleanor's team and members of the church ministry team started to pray, people began to fall in the power of the Spirit. Soon the whole church was affected. There were scenes that few had ever seen before. The children arrived from their own groups and many of them were deeply touched and began praying for each other. Prayers went on well past 1.30.

At the evening service the scenes were repeated and the prayers continued for more than an hour and a half. By the Tuesday, news was coming in of other London churches being affected by a similar outpouring of the Holy Spirit, including the Holy Trinity 'plant', St Paul's, Onslow Square.

Meanwhile, such was the extent of what was taking place that Sandy Millar, the Holy Trinity vicar and Jeremy Jennings, pastoral director, decided to fly to Toronto for a three-day visit. There they met John Peters, of St Paul's, Onslow Square, some members of St Stephen's, Twickenham, and pastors from all over the world anxious to see and experience what God was doing.

On the following Sunday, 5 June, Sandy Millar asked Nicky Gumbel and members of the congregation who had been touched by the Holy Spirit the previous week to say what had happened to them. Soon the Holy Spirit was falling upon people all over the church. Such was the impact upon so many people that the planned Communion service could not go ahead.

The evening service was packed with some 1,200 people. Sandy Millar again invited people to come forward to say what God had been doing to them. One young man said that he was suffering from AIDS and had come to the church just recently. He had never experienced such love as he had at Holy Trinity at that time.

*

Sandy Millar, vicar of Holy Trinity, Brompton, wrote to his congregation: We have begun to see an astonishing outpouring of the Spirit of God upon our own church and congregation. It seems to be a spontaneous work of the Holy Spirit and there are certainly some very surprising manifestations of the Spirit excitingly reminiscent of accounts of early revivals and movements of God's Spirit.

Some of the manifestations include: prolonged laughter, totally unselfconscious for the most part, and an inexpressible and glorious joy (1 Pet 1.8). For some it is prolonged weeping and crying and a sense of conviction and desire for forgiveness, purity and peace with God. For others it seems to be the silent reception of the Spirit of God sometimes leading to falling down and sometimes standing up, sometimes kneeling, sometimes sitting.

There are great varieties of the manifestations of the Spirit. They are breaking out both during services and outside them in homes and offices. At times they are easy to explain and handle and at other times they are much harder and more complicated.

We had been hearing for several days of the movement of God's Spirit in the Vineyard Church in Toronto, Canada, and a number of people have come to us from there telling us about what was going on and of what they thought it all meant. For that reason Jeremy Jennings and I decided to go briefly to Toronto to see what we could learn and what conclusions, if any, at this stage it was possible to draw. The manifestations are quite extraordinary and would undoubtedly be alarming if we had not read about them previously in history.

The manifestations themselves of course are not as significant as the working of the Spirit of God in the individual and the church. The manifestations are the signs and therefore of course it is to the fruit that we look rather than the signs.

The church in Toronto first experienced these signs on 20 January and since then has been ministering to an increasing number of outside people: ministers and church members from all over America, Canada, now Europe and even further afield. Meetings go on night after night (every night except Monday) and include a pastors' meeting on a Wednesday from 12.00 to roughly 3.30 in the afternoon.

Their understanding is that God seems to be pouring out his Spirit, refreshing his people and drawing them closer to himself, revealing his love to them and a deep sense of preciousness in a way that kindles their own sense of the love of God, their love for Scripture, and their desire to be involved in the activities of the Spirit of God today. So this is primarily a movement towards God's people.

Naturally we expect it to flow out and over into a movement that will affect the rest of the world but for the moment it's God's deep desire to minister to his church – to refresh, empower, and prepare it for a wider work of his Spirit that will affect the world to which the church is sent.

I think it's important that we should stay close to the Lord and be grateful for every sign of his grace upon us. Don't let us get too caught up with the signs of his Spirit but more with him and his love for us.

Let's encourage those who think they have experienced nothing (it may or may not be true) – and let's above all continue to pray that through this outpouring of God's Spirit he will build a church worthy of him: holy, equipped and full of love and grace towards him and the outside world. Meanwhile let's pray that it may continue. And continue to pray for one another.

Two members of Holy Trinity, Brompton, describe what happened when the Holy Spirit fell.

Roland Travis is a group leader: When I arrived at the evening service, I was feeling very frustrated and filled with pent-up anger to do with my work. When Sandy Millar started praying for everyone to be filled with the Holy Spirit, I felt my arms starting to move. Then all my limbs started to move. The first time I 'went down', I felt all the anger go. After that I felt the Holy Spirit was on me for the rest of the evening. When I was praying for people my arms kept moving and I couldn't stop them. I feel closer to God.

Emmy Wilson is a member of staff: When Nicky Gumbel prayed, the Holy Spirit came in power on all of us. I just felt I was falling in love with the Lord all over again. There was some excited sort of crying out to Jesus. One moment I was laughing and the next minute I was just weeping and weeping before the Lord. Into my mind came people who didn't know the Lord or who were not filled with the Spirit. I was crying out that he would not miss anybody out. That was the cry from my heart.

3

Fresh outpourings of the Holy Spirit

As he heard increasing reports of outpourings of the Holy Spirit across many nations and groups of churches, **Terry Virgo** found himself living through some of the most extraordinary days of his Christian life.

It all began when I returned to the church that I am presently serving in Columbia, Missouri, after a two-week visit to South Africa. On my return I found that God had begun to do a new, wonderful work among the people. The repercussions are still being worked out.

I found that our church meetings were totally transformed and that a new release of the power of the Holy Spirit had overtaken us. People testified to wonderful changes in their lives.

God has been visiting our meetings in remarkable ways and we have been thrilled to see extraordinary sights in terms of people being filled with the Holy Spirit and with joy and 'drunkenness'. We have seen so many lives totally transformed. People have a new hunger for God and a new zeal to see him glorified. Bad relationships have been healed and weak marriages have been wonderfully strengthened. Formerly depressed people have been changed beyond recognition.

I have never seen such rapid change in individual lives and in the whole atmosphere of a church. I am so glad that, from the beginning, I saw substantial spiritual fruit in the lives of those affected. The immediate manifestations were so strange, but the continuing impact on people's lives has been magnificent.

One of the most remarkable occasions in our recent church life was when a visiting speaker was about to address the people. As he read his opening remarks, the power of God swept through the building totally unrelated to the words that he had said, which actually were rather serious and sombre.

His opening remarks were, 'The story of Solomon is one of the most tragic in the whole Bible.' This sober comment was greeted by sudden outbursts of hilarious laughter from several people in the meeting. I was, of course, initially embarrassed that our visiting speaker should be so greeted.

After a while it became apparent there was no way that we could stop this spontaneous, uninvited laughter. The visiting speaker, though at first perplexed, proceeded to invite those who had been affected by the Spirit to come forward, which they did. When they arrived at the front of the church building, they were overwhelmed by God and fell to the ground in convulsive laughter.

The meeting continued until 11.30 at night with no opportunity for the speaker to preach, and with scores and scores of people having powerful meetings with God. People began laying hands on one another, but would sometimes find themselves affected more than the one they prayed for. It was extremely difficult to organise this outbreak of God's presence. Indeed there was no organisation at all but a mighty and spontaneous outpouring, with many falling helplessly to the floor.

A few days later I returned to England and found that wherever I went to report this outbreak, God accompanied us with more signs of his mercy and overwhelming love for his church.

First I met with a number of ministers who help me in leading New Frontiers and we had two days of amazing experiences of God's presence and a release of prophesying such as I have never known. Some of the brothers were once again overwhelmed with laughter and 'drunkenness', a joy which could not be contained.

Then came my return to my home church in Brighton, where I had heard that a fresh move of the Spirit had begun early in May following a powerful prophecy in February warning us to be prepared for God's disruption. We had an unforgettable evening together which continued until nearly midnight. Many were overwhelmed by the power of the Holy Spirit.

I simply stood to describe what had happened in the USA and invited those who were thirsty for a fresh touch from God to come to the front of the meeting place. About 200 people came forward. Before I could explain what I was about to do, two men fell to the ground laughing uncontrollably, and then the Holy Spirit broke out all over the room. Once again, we continued simply to pray for one another but often the Holy Spirit came upon people before we reached them.

Following this, over 200 full-time ministers from churches within the New Frontiers family of churches gathered for a two-day prayer conference. But once again, the Holy Spirit was poured out in a phenomenal way characterised by extraordinary 'drunkenness' and a release of mighty prophesying of breathtaking proportions. The events of those two days will be stamped indelibly on the memories of all who attended. Hours sped by as we prayed, prophesied and worshipped.

We had not only gathered from the 100 English New Frontiers churches but had also invited home Duncan Watkinson, who oversees our churches in the Middle East and India, and Simon Pettit, who oversees the New Frontiers churches in South Africa.

Following their return, there have been identical stories of the outbreak of the power of God, some people becoming so 'drunk' with the Holy Spirit that they had to be carried home from meetings. The outbreak even took place in Christian congregations in the predominantly Muslim Middle East nations and also in the different language congregations in Bombay. Upon his return to Cape Town, Simon Pettit reported that they had never had such a weekend.

On my return to Missouri, we had a leadership retreat with over 300 leaders from churches with which I am working. Once again God's power was released. Joy and exuberance mingled with powerful prophecy and strong intercession while the sense of God's presence in worship was sometimes overwhelming. Again, people were so 'drunk' that they had to be escorted back to their rooms.

I have often quoted the scripture 'These men are not drunk as you suppose,' but in the past, I have applied it almost exclusively to the manifestation of speaking in tongues. Now I have seen many people totally 'drunk' in the Holy Spirit. Many are overwhelmed with laughter and cannot walk, who are carried, who sing extraordinary songs, and who are filled with amazing love for Jesus. I have seen lives radically changed at phenomenal speed. For some, their laughter is preceded by tears and crying out to God whereupon their sorrow is turned to joy and their tears into laughter.

Two things have been particularly impressed upon me during these weeks. Firstly, the amazing grace of God in giving this spiritual breakthrough. God's blessings are absolutely free. The doctrine of God's grace is wonderfully underlined in our hearts and in our experience. In the past some have spoken of 'paying the price' for an outpouring of the Holy Spirit, but I have to say that it was Jesus who paid the price of the outpouring of the Spirit on the day of Pentecost and he has paid the price for every subsequent outpouring.

Secondly, I feel that the Lord spoke to me recently and said, 'I have attended many of your meetings, now I am inviting you to attend some of mine!' As a preacher who puts a very high value on Bible exposition, I have to acknowledge that people who have met with God powerfully in these meetings are more changed than when listening to me preach. So I am learning respectfully to 'get out of the way' when the Holy Spirit wants to break out upon us, though Bible teaching still plays a key role.

I certainly embrace this as an authentic move of the Holy Spirit. Sometimes in public meetings statements are made, the doctrinal foundations of which leave me with disquiet, but that does not take away from the reality of this mighty expression of the power of God among his people.

My perspective is that I will drink and encourage others to drink while I will also see it as my responsibility to teach the Word and feed biblical truth into the midst of this wonderful stirring of the Spirit of God. I urge all who read my words to keep an open heart to what God is doing and come thirsty and desirous to meet with God.

Who knows how far this move of the Spirit will go and how much it is preparatory to a great revival move from God such as the mighty outpourings taking place at present in China and Argentina sweeping thousands into the Kingdom of God. Keep praying that it may be so.

*

The Holy Spirit hits Hope Valley

Meanwhile, in Hope Valley in South Australia, Brian Anderson with his wife Thora and a 10-strong ministry team, all from North Phoenix Vineyard, visited the parish church. The minister, the **Rev Dr Graham Twelftree** describes how 'the Spirit fell on us as I have never seen before on such a large scale . . .'

There were 200–300 people at each of the nightly meetings. At the end of his talks Brian Anderson conducted a time of ministry. He asked those who wanted a touch from the Lord to stand. Almost everyone seemed to stand. There were too many for us and the team to reach so they were asked to come to the front.

There were dozens and dozens of people lying on the floor every night, weeping, chuckling, laughing loudly, groaning, a few screaming, many gently rocking or swaying and some shaking; one young man stood shaking for over an hour. Others staggered as if drunk. Some lay on the floor motionless for up to an hour, sometimes more. Two or three had to be taken out to have demons exorcised from them or deep emotional issues dealt with. I would wander among the dozens of folk who had come to the front and pray quietly next to them or gently touch them. They would be overcome by the presence of God, so had to be lowered quickly on to the floor.

One night I saw a middle-aged man sit up after he had fallen down. Noticing his wife a few feet away, he crawled over to her on all fours. Tears of joy and peace came to their eyes as they embraced on the floor. A few old people had chairs hurriedly brought to them so they could sit, resting or shaking gently for half an hour or so.

Paul, our son, 'went down' and was laid across some chairs for an hour or so. As a team member walked past Paul, the word 'songs' came to his mind. He prayed about this with Paul, who went home and wrote out parts of six songs.

A young man in his twenties attempted to get up from the floor but could not. All he could do was to lift his head and look around. He told us God had said that, while at present he was being obedient to him in his life, if he did not continue in that obedience, this would be his condition. It may have been 20 minutes or more before he could get up.

One story bears telling at length. A long-haired, bearded man in his thirties, 22 years addicted to drugs, who had been in our building only a few times, was pointed out to me. I went over and asked him a question to discover whether or not he meant business with God. I suggested he held out his hands in front of him as if to receive from God. I said that if what I prayed made sense to him and it was what he wanted to say to God, he could make them his own words in his mind. His right hand began to shake from side to side. Much perspiration appeared all over his face, and his body – through his clothes – was hot to touch. His nose began to run and water dripped continuously out of his eyes. A number of times I had to wipe his face, nose and beard. Then he seemed to get shorter and shorter as his knees gave way. Eventually he fell back. But his neck was tense and his head did not fall back.

I asked if there was something in particular I could pray for. 'My addiction – drugs.' I prayed a little more and his head dropped back into my hand and I rested it on the floor. Two men were praying with me and a few others were close by praying. We all continued praying for five or ten minutes more. Then he opened his eyes and sat up, crossing his legs. I lay down on the floor to look up into his face. He was clearly a refreshed, different, if exhausted, person. I beckoned to his wife – herself a new Christian with an incredible story – to come over. She was crying with joy as they sat embracing on the floor.

On the following Monday they came to see me. He brought a bin bag of cannabis and his pipe to hand over to me. We chatted and prayed. He was quite different. From taking drugs a dozen times a day, he had now taken none.

Over Sunday, we had our usual three services. There were a few extra in the morning services (212 in the 9.00 and 261 in the 10.45) but double the number at the 6.30 (452), making 925 through the day. In each of the services, as during the week, a third to half of the chairs had to be removed to make room for those being ministered to by the Spirit. At the end of the evening service, people of all ages rejoiced. Dozens gathered around the team from America to lay hands on them and give them farewell hugs. I find myself weeping with joy as I write, so grateful to God that he has come here in such a powerful and life-changing way.

There is a sense of joy, peace and wonder at what God has done. There is a sense of anticipation at what seems to be a new beginning for us. Our response needs to be a greater desire for holiness, a longing to maintain the love and unity brought and a passion for those who do not know God.

4

The Holy Spirit in our midst

Hundreds of churches throughout Britain became affected by the movement of the Holy Spirit during the summer of 1994. At Millmead Centre, Guildford, pastoral leader **Peter Nodding** gave this account of what was happening there.

Peter Jackson and Chris Scupham from Millmead had booked into a day's conference at St Andrew's, Chorleywood on 16 June, addressing the subject of working in the community. They followed this theme in the morning, but in the afternoon Bishop David Pytches, who had recently returned from Toronto, shared what had happened to him.

Peter and Chris were both touched by the Spirit, one with liberating laughter and the other with the weight of the Spirit resting upon him. The next day I was prayed for. Since then we have been experiencing the anointing of the Spirit at elders' and deacons' meetings, in small groups and in the main services.

What are the main features?

I will mention five:

Tears: These are very common when the Spirit is at work so I need not comment.

Laughter: On the last couple of Sundays we have experienced laughter (or holy joy) in the main services. Why laughter? It is the joy of the Lord. It is a way in which God shares his own joy with us. I am sure all of you have at times laughed helplessly and felt so much better for it. In this case there is no one telling jokes, in fact humanly there is no substance to the laughter. However it brings us closer to the Lord, and is spiritually therapeutic. The laughter comes and goes as the Lord releases waves of his Spirit.

Shaking: This is not new. The Quakers were the shakers, that is why they received their name. A number of us have experienced this involuntary shaking.

The weight of the Spirit: The power of the Spirit is coming upon us. It usually means that we need to sit or lie down. The level of weight will vary from person to person. In most cases I believe people could remain standing up, but it would mean coming out of what the Spirit is doing. You remember Ezekiel spoke several times of 'the strong hand of the Lord upon me'.

Heavy breathing accompanied sometimes with bodily movements.

All these experiences are not causing us to be afraid. Indeed, on the contrary, they are giving a sense of the love and acceptance of God. What is actually happening? As the power of the Spirit comes upon us, we are responding. I understand the reactions mentioned above to be our spiritual, emotional and physical response to the power of the Spirit. As a result of infusions and anointings of the Spirit our human frame can be overwhelmed and so reacts. God is spirit and is demonstrating his love and power among us. We need have no fear of what comes from the Lord.

What is the fruit of this so far?

A greater passion for Jesus. I observe in myself and others that the person of Jesus has become even more precious to us. We can be reassured that this is a move of the Spirit of God because he is highlighting the wonder and significance of his Son. You will know the several places in Scripture where we are told that the Holy Spirit will glorify Jesus.

An accelerated growth in sanctification/holiness: I mean in the sense of setting ourselves apart for the Lord. Some deeper changes may take longer to be evidenced.

Some people have asked where is the repentance in this move of the Spirit? They have been especially worried about the laughter. But what is the fruit of repentance? It is a change of attitude about God. It is to be consumed with the things of God rather than the things of earth or self. It is wanting to live in the way that Jesus did, in humanity and obedience. These attitudes are at the heart of this refreshing for many of us.

An accelerated growth in spiritual gifts: With the new anointing of the Holy Spirit comes the more natural flow of his gifts, including prophecy, words of knowledge and healing. This is, of course, going to be true because, when we are giving freedom to the Spirit, he will automatically distribute his gifts. This is what he wants to do all of the time.

Allied to this I have heard that some members have been wonderfully set free in Christ. Personal difficulties, that might usually take several counselling appointments to resolve, are being healed in a much shorter time. The Lord is also unearthing aspects of our lives with which he wishes to deal.

A greater capacity to 'carry' the work of God: It is as though we know more of what he wants to accomplish and have a greater faith and boldness to see it through. (I am referring to God enabling us to carry his work in the power of his Spirit.) These won't be the only things that the Spirit is doing.

Is this for everyone?

The first point to make is that God loves all of us exactly the same. His aim is to bless all of us deeply. It won't happen for all of us at the same time, so let us rejoice in those who are receiving and be encouraged by it. Not all of us are going to have the same manifestations. In fact, what is the most important is what the Lord is doing inside us, not the outward.

Let us not measure how powerfully the Spirit is at work by how dramatic the manifestations are. As our friend Ken McGreavy often says, 'It is not manifestation that is most important, it is transformation.' The long-term fruit is the best test.

However, God must have more of his Spirit for all of us. Only you will know whether or not you are receiving more from him. Just as all of us needed to receive Christ, we all need to go on receiving his Spirit. For this to be the case there will need to be an openness and a growing hunger for the Lord.

Where is it all going?

I believe that it is a preparation for a move of the Spirit in the country. Leaders have been saying for some time that we are nearer to a move that will affect the nation. So it is not revival at this stage. The Lord is equipping his church with more of himself. The leaders here at Millmead want to lead with both spiritual and common sense. We believe that what is coming to us is the answer to our prayers.

How many of you have prayed for the Lord to send his Spirit? Let us now rejoice that he is doing just that. We will be wise and open to the way in which he wants to be active among us. We will be listening to the Lord and will be seeking his direction to open the doors to the fullness of his blessing here.

What do we have to do?

Seek the Lord: Not only keep our eyes on him, but actively seek him; to seek him for himself. It is to ask for more hunger and thirst. It is those who hunger and thirst after righteousness who will be filled.

Relax: God is unlikely to do something to you if you don't want it. However, often there is ambivalence within us. In our hearts we want more from God, but in our heads we don't. Thank God, he reads our heart and works in us anyway.

Allow others to receive in church services: There are folk who want to be prayed for and let us rejoice with them. In this season of refreshing the only way that we can provide this ministry is by giving time on Sundays. We will do this sensitively and will be faithful to God the Spirit. So if you find yourself reacting negatively or being resistant, try to submit to the Lord and ask him to help you.

Pray that God will keep us in tune with him: There are clearly dangers with any move of the Spirit. But the answer isn't to quench him but to ask for more of him, because the more we have of him, the less we have of ourselves. Just as years ago when folk were getting uptight about spiritual gifts, the answer wasn't no use, but right use. The Lord loves us so much. We are safer in his hands that in our own. The Lord wants to keep us in the flow of his love and power. Through his grace it can be so.

*

Spirit power in South Wales

The Covenant Life Church in Cardiff meets in the All Nations Centre, which has a 1,000-seat auditorium and excellent facilities. It is the church's own centre. It has cost £1.25 million, of which only £400 remains to be paid. The church itself raised the money.

The vision of a centre with such a capacity was a foreshadowing of what has been happening in the power of the Holy Spirit. Covenant Life Church has become a focal point of the renewal which is happening in a number of churches in the area. Its Wednesday night meetings have been drawing up to 500 visitors. Some are from other churches; some are not Christians but come because they want to be.

The normal programme of church activities was scrapped to allow the Holy Spirit to operate freely. 'We prayed, looked into the Scriptures and waited on God,' said Peter Greasley, a church elder. People have been leaving the meetings 'drunk' with the Spirit. There have been many healings. Outsiders have been coming to personal faith in Christ at each meeting.

'The ABC of evangelism has gone out of the window,' said Peter Greasley. He gave as an example the conversion of the mother of a house-group leader. She had fallen to the floor under the power of the Holy Spirit. When she stood up, she was asked, 'Do you want to give your life to Christ?' 'I feel I have already,' she replied.

Three men with an unsavoury background came to one of the meetings. They had been involved with drugs. All three came under strong conviction, sought forgiveness and experienced God's blessing. They were baptised there and then. This is normal at Covenant Life Church, which has a pool filled with warm water all ready.

'It's a joy to be linked with other churches in renewal,' said Peter Greasley. Woodville Road Baptist Church cancelled its own mid-week meeting to join in with Covenant Life. Lisvanne Baptist Church and the Elim City Temple are two other local churches to have been touched by the Holy Spirit, as well as several Anglican churches.

Four hundred leading members of churches in Cardiff, Newport and the surrounding area were invited to the All Nations Centre for a training day and to report and discuss recent events.

A man arrived at Covenant Life Church from Ammanford, some 50 miles away. He told Peter Greasley that God had shown his face in a vision. He described how his grandfather had been saved on the street through Evan Roberts during the Welsh revival of 1904. Hearing of what had been happening at present, he exclaimed, 'All that you have been telling me is the same as my grandfather used to describe.'

5

'A season of glorious disorder'

The phrase, borrowed from C H Spurgeon, the great 19th-century preacher, aptly sums up the move of the Holy Spirit among leaders and members of the King's Church, Aldershot. **John Peters** reports.

A season of glorious disorder is how Derek Brown, leader of the King's Church, characterises recent events in the church. In quite extraordinary ways, people have been affected as perhaps never before in the history of the King's Church, which moved to its present site, a renovated former cinema, in 1984.

In February 1994, in Godalming, at a church in close relationship with Aldershot, Derek Brown felt led to preach on the joy of the Lord. This resulted in a significant release of the Spirit, including irrepressible laughter. A similar response occurred when he preached the same sermon in Aldershot and also in Scotland, where there was phenomenal 'drunkenness' in the Spirit.

The impetus was maintained in May at a conference of leaders associated with the King's Church, Aldershot. A particular and unusual feature of this conference was the sight of grown men crying out to God in confession of their sins to one another.

Thus far, only sporadic stirrings had been observed, but soon the situation was to change dramatically. It was evident in the morning meeting on Sunday 19 June that the Holy Spirit was powerfully at work, which created a feeling of expectancy. Events in the evening service were more remarkable, with a perfectly routine baptismal occasion turning out rather differently. People were slain in the Spirit both before and as they were baptised, and the meeting continued unabated until almost 2am on Monday.

For the next three weeks, by which time the church had heard of the Toronto blessing, the church met each evening except Saturdays, and subsequently three times weekly, with no apparent let-up in the momentum. One damp Wednesday in August, for example, 400 people gathered together, eager to receive more of God's power and in-filling.

The phenomena witnessed in the King's Church, Aldershot, have much in common with those at other large south-east England churches such as Church of Christ the King, Brighton, and Holy Trinity, Brompton, in London, to name but two, including: falling down as though dead (Rev 1.17); laughter and joy (Ps 65.8; 126.2); 'drunkenness' (Ac 2.13–15; Eph 5.18); trembling (Dan 10.10–11; 1 Cor 2.3) and groaning in the Spirit (Rom 8.22–23).

In addition, a number of people were quite literally 'frozen' and unable to move. One woman in her late forties said rather bemusedly, 'I was blessed by the Spirit without even asking.'

Some were so 'drunk' in the Spirit that they were unable to walk. Others were so overwhelmed by the Spirit's revelations to them that they wept for long periods. The experience of unusual manifestations has gone from old to young people, right down to young children.

Some church members have recoiled at the intensity of events, others have maintained that what is happening is not of God and may be satanic. Undeniably there has been evidence of fleshly behaviour, with some people courting attention out of their emotional, psychological or religious needs. Also, some people have acted in bizarre ways or given 'words' or visions which have been out of tune with what the Spirit has been trying to do.

Equally undeniably, there has been a deep and authentic move of God in the lives of many, many Christians, a high proportion of whom are mature and balanced men and women with many years of exposure to charismatic gifts of the Holy Spirit. It is most unlikely that group suggestion, or hysteria, or attention-seeking is the reason for the wholehearted involvement of such people in what is happening, still less for their keen desire to embrace this latest outpouring of God's Spirit. It is more likely that, genuinely and passionately, they desire God to revive them individually, the church collectively and Britain nationally.

It is not just manifestations that have been apparent in the church. It is also possible to point to discernible fruit in the lives of individuals and the church as a whole. Some aspects of the evident fruit in the lives of men, women and children may be mentioned.

Large numbers of people have been sensitised to sin in their lives, but not so much the more overt sins like lying, gossiping, cheating, or sexual promiscuity. It has been a deep conviction of the apathy that is so prevalent among western Christians today. In this sort of rut, everything is predictable, vision is absent, expectancy is lacking, evangelism diminishes and a loathsome self-righteousness takes over, together with complacency and self-satisfaction about our spiritual condition. Recent events in Aldershot have alerted people to the perils of such a condition. A number of people have been quite forcibly shaken out of their spiritual torpor and lack of zeal. A deep awareness of sin – in all its varied forms – has historically been the prelude to revival in the fullest sense: it is the hope of the King's Church, Aldershot.

To compare tapes of the worship before and after Sunday 19 June is instructive. Before that day, the worship is lively, even quite creative. Since that day it has an impact, an anointing, that is not dependent on the suitability of the songs chosen, the skill of the musicians, or the sensitivity of the worship leader.

Quite simply, it has glimpses of heaven, of glory, with a joy that is the fruit of relationship: people communing with God, not just singing; praising, not just going through the motions; worshipping as opposed to 'doing' the worship bit as a prelude to the sermon.

Confession: one young woman confessed to an adulterous affair which her husband knew nothing about. Others made confession of obsessive behaviour, like the young mother of a daughter with various disabilities: 'I felt so much the love and gentleness of the Lord when I was delivered from grief over my child's mental and physical condition. Also, over the past few weeks I have lost my obsession with television completely and I've lost eight pounds in weight, because I don't have to "comfort eat" any more.'

Restitution: a woman in her mid-twenties had stolen from her employer and made full restitution of what she had taken.

Release: for one young man, the events of recent days have accelerated God's process of changing his life: 'God has been slowly but surely changing me. My heart has become softer, my mind clearer, and my conviction of Christ as my Lord and Saviour stronger than ever. . . . It has happened through the power of God. My background is one of a lonely, greedy and selfish individual who became hardened to the world. But now my mind is being renewed and my spirit is caused to be at peace.'

Healings: both emotional and physical healings have occurred. One woman suffering extreme pain in her left shoulder was unable to lift her arm at all. After a period of resting in the Spirit on the floor, she started flexing the muscles of her hand: 'I persevered and I could feel the shoulder becoming free of pain and I could lift it high. By the time I got home all pain and stiffness had gone.'

Another woman, who is confined to a wheelchair, was released from the pain of losing her legs and additionally was 'filled with laughter'. Another person was healed of ME.

There has also been deep emotional healing in the lives of many people, neuroses dealt with, psychological hurts of long-standing cured, marriages restored, broken relationships put back together. Truly our God is one who heals.

Is it revival? Definitions are particularly important when considering a word like revival. It is often confused with renewal, evangelism, the restoration of back-slidden or apathetic Christians, or with 'an unusual sense of God's presence hovering over a congregation for a period of time' (Selwyn Hughes).

Current events in the King's Church, Aldershot, and those as elsewhere reported, do not constitute revival. There are supernatural signs and some extraordinary, even spectacular, events. But few people would dare assert that the Lord Jesus has been restored to his rightful place as Lord of the church.

At present the outpouring is confined to the church itself, though encouragingly it is taking place right across the denominational spectrum. Certainly we are witnessing 'times of refreshing' from God, and the King's Church is part of something supernatural world-wide.

Put conservatively, it is an inkling of what happens on a much larger scale in revival; a foretaste, a prelude, and as such is to be eagerly welcomed, though constantly reviewed in the light of the teaching of Scripture.

It is the fervent hope of all connected with the King's Church in Aldershot and its associated churches that, soon, God will sweep in, bringing the blaze and glory of revival to Britain and the world.

6

The preacher who was humbled

Friday evenings at Westminster Chapel have been a special time
of Bible teaching throughout this century. Wallace Boulton
went there to hear how **Dr R T Kendall** is continuing the
tradition in his own way. It was surprising what else emerged in
the interview . . .

I was a little early for my appointment at Westminster Chapel
with Dr R T Kendall. So I wandered from the lounge into the
chapel, emerging just behind the large pulpit, encircled by its
polished wooden balustrade. Surely there is not a bigger pulpit
in Britain. As the focal point of the building, it symbolises the
tradition of outstanding preaching and teaching which has for
so long characterised Westminster Chapel.

This is where Campbell Morgan preached at the start of the
century. It is where Dr Martyn Lloyd-Jones, popularly known as
the Doctor', held sway for so many years. He was succeeded in
1977 by the present minister, Dr R T Kendall. He came to England
from Kentucky in 1973 to study at Oxford, where he received his
doctorate in 1976. Known simply as 'R T' ('right theology' he
quips), he has been making his own distinctive mark as a biblical
expositor, not only at Westminster Chapel but at Spring Harvest
and Keswick and through his books.

Dr Kendall had joined me now and we went up into the pulpit
together and stood behind the well-worn black ledge for the

preacher's notes. Beside it, adding a modern touch, was a white intercom phone.

'Paul Cain stood beside me here,' said R T. 'He hadn't been to Westminster Chapel before. He gazed out at the rows of pews and said he saw a great revival coming. We have had five such clear prophecies. They have not yet been fulfilled, but I really do believe that a spiritual awakening is coming to Britain. I also believe that God will use those who have been equipped, who have been trained and who will have gone to the trouble to learn things.'

R T Kendall is convinced that such teaching is even more needed by today's Christians. His distinctive contribution is the School of Theology on Friday evenings.

'It's the most successful thing I've done in nearly 18 years here,' he said. 'This will be our third year. We have a few more coming each time. Probably 80 per cent of those who have come keep coming.'

He stressed the importance of knowledge. 'In John 14.26, Jesus said that the Holy Spirit would remind us of what he had taught them. Well, if there is nothing there to be reminded of, it doesn't matter how filled with the Spirit you are. If you are empty-headed before you are Spirit-filled, you will be empty-headed afterwards.

'Do you know, Scripture memorisation has almost perished from the earth? Many people are bored with teaching, bored with preaching. I can understand, because there's a lot of boring preaching and teaching around. But this is a pity, because our people need to be theologically equipped and this is where I seek to come in.'

R T Kendall is a very candid, open person, as I had discovered when he shared details of his childhood and his relationship with his father with 4,000 Christians in the Big Top at Spring Harvest. He was equally frank when he came to discuss the 'Toronto experience' and its arrival here.

'I have had to make a public climbdown,' he admitted. 'If you had put me on a lie detector when I first heard about it, and asked me if I thought this was of God, I would have said no. Two weeks later I changed my mind. I saw one of my closest friends, who wasn't all that open to it, fall flat on his face for 10 or 15 minutes when he was prayed for in my vestry.

'The man who prayed for my friend had come to pray for me, which he did. But my friend said he would allow himself to be prayed for, not expecting anything to happen. He had only heard of Toronto that morning from me. He was the one who fell flat on the floor, not me. That impressed me.'

The next day R T had lunch with Ken Costa, a churchwarden at Holy Trinity, Brompton. 'I knew in my heart that the things he was telling me had to be of God,' he affirmed. On the following Sunday he was frank with his congregation. He said from the pulpit, 'I have been preaching here for years. If the Holy Spirit would come with power at All Souls, Langham Place, or Kensington Temple, would we have the integrity to affirm it?'

'Mind you,' he told me, 'I never thought I would have to do it. But I have publicly affirmed what is happening at Holy Trinity, Brompton.

'We are grateful for what God is doing elsewhere and, we hope, in Westminster Chapel as well. It may be that that is not what God is calling us to do, but I can tell you we are open to it. We will be a bit disappointed if we don't get into it up to the hilt.'

He had led prayers for Sandy Millar, vicar of Holy Trinity, Brompton, and then invited him to come with six of his people to address the deacons and their wives at Westminster Chapel, to minister to them. Dr Kendall went on to speak with complete openness about his own experience.

'I had been prayed for by a number of people. Sandy Millar was the first, then Roger Forster and Ken Costa and two or three others from the staff of Holy Trinity, Brompton. Nothing happened. My wife joined us as they were praying for me. After about two minutes she was on the floor. I had never seen such a radiant smile on her face. She wept, she laughed, and she said to me later that if this was what being slain in the Spirit was, she could see why people wanted it.

'Then, on the evening that Sandy Millar and his staff came to our church, we were about to go home when one of them asked if he could pray for me. I said, "Sure, but I must tell you I've been prayed for many times." I didn't want him to get his hopes up.

'Within a minute or so, suddenly my mind became so relaxed. The nearest I can think of to describe it was when I had sodium pentathol years ago when I had major surgery. Yet I wasn't unconscious. I felt myself falling forward.'

Did he have a great sense of God? 'No more than I had felt all day; it had been a great day for me.' What, then, was the meaning of this experience? 'For me, it was so humbling. I think God was wanting to teach me to be humbled, to look stupid and to be a fool. There I was on the floor in front of all my deacons and their wives. There were only a couple of others to whom it happened that evening and I was embarrassed. I think that was what God wanted to do to me.'

7

'Toronto' and Scripture

The 'Toronto experience' has been questioned in some Christian circles. Is it biblical? **Gerald Coates** offers a robust response to the doubters.

One of the most frequently asked questions, particularly from conservative evangelicals, is 'Where is all this in the Bible?' They are of course referring to convulsive laughter, weeping and deep sobbing, shaking and trembling and people prostrate before the Lord or flat on their backs. The last-named state is sometimes accompanied by a feeling of loss of control and an inability to get up. In the words of Jonathan Edwards, 'Bodily strength is withdrawn.' In other situations people are well able to get up but feel it right to stay down.

There is plenty of biblical material covering these manifestations of the Holy Spirit and reactions to his presence. Some may regard biblical evidence for these manifestations as either slim or scarce. But it is well accepted, within biblical scholarship and evangelical circles, that the importance of an issue cannot be gauged by the number of times it is mentioned. For example, 'born again' is mentioned only two or three times in the entire New Testament. The breaking of bread is referred to on a handful of occasions.

Before we look at some of the manifestations of the Spirit, or people responding to the Spirit, it should also be noted that the

Bible is not given so that we can provide a proof text for everything. Most Christians are currently engaged in a wide range of church activities for which there are no proof texts.

There are things God approves of in Scripture, and we call them scriptural; there are things God disapproves of in Scripture, and we call them unscriptural; but there are many things that are plainly non-scriptural. We draw our experiences alongside Scripture to test them to see whether they are of God or not.

Things most Christians are involved in without much biblical data to support them include church buildings, the gospel preached to the converted at 6.30 every Sunday evening, closing your eyes when you pray, saying grace before meals, Sunday schools, youth clubs, women's meetings, and even a daily morning quiet time.

That is not to say these things are wrong. The point I am making is that God wants us to grow up. Between those things he specifically approves of, and others he specifically disapproves of, we are given liberty to develop a wide range of activities broadly to reflect things he approves of. The same liberty applies to manifestations of the Holy Spirit's presence. Scripture gives more than sufficient evidence and endorsement for the following responses.

Trembling/shaking: 'My flesh trembles for fear of thee and I am afraid of thy judgment' (Ps 119.120). 'Worship the Lord with reverence and rejoice with trembling' (Ps 2.11). The apostle Paul was deeply affected while he was with the church in Corinth: 'I was with you in weakness and in fear and in much trembling' (1 Cor 2.3).

When Paul and Timothy wrote to the church in Philippi they told them to 'work out your salvation with fear and trembling' (Phil 2.12). Indeed (even in the Old Testament) the expected response from those who realised they were in the presence of God was clear. 'Do you not fear me?, declares the Lord. Do you not tremble in my presence?' (Jer 5.22).

Weeping: interestingly, in our own church, Pioneer People (situated between Guildford and Kingston), we have had more weeping than laughing. In May 1990 it was prophesied that our church would be marked by weeping. This had not happened to any great extent before then. The scripture around which this prophecy hung was: 'Now while Ezra was praying and making confession, weeping and prostrating himself before the house of the Lord, a very large assembly, men, women and children, gathered to him from Israel; for the people wept bitterly' (Ez 10.1). Nehemiah the governor and Ezra the priest and scribe, along with the Levites, actually discouraged the people: 'Do not mourn or weep,' they said (Neh 8.9).

Weeping is often a sign of maturity and sensitivity to one's own personal sin or the needs around us. A compassionate heart is often marked by tears, even in the unconverted. Tears of joy and gratitude were prophesied by Jeremiah when prophecy was to be fulfilled. 'With weeping they shall come, and by supplication I will lead them; I will make them walk on streams of water, on a straight path in which they shall not stumble' (Jer 31.9). Joel invites the people of God to return to God 'with fasting, weeping and mourning' (Joel 2.12).

John, Jesus' best friend, exiled on Patmos, gives future hope to the crushed and bereaved. 'He shall wipe away every tear from their eyes; and there shall no longer be any death; there shall no longer be any mourning, or crying, or pain: the first things have passed away' (Rev 21.4).

Appearing drunk/trance-like: on the day of Pentecost 120 people were filled with the Holy Spirit, spoke in tongues, made a noise and as a result a crowd gathered. Some, mocking, observed, 'They are full of sweet wine' (Ac 2.13).

Peter responded, 'These men are not drunk, as you suppose, for it is only 9am' (Ac 2.15). There was something about their behaviour that was so bizarre, out of the ordinary or unco-ordinated that it led people to believe they were drunk.

Eli thought Hannah was drunk (1 Sam 1.13). Saul certainly appeared unusual (if not drunk) when he 'stripped off his clothes . . . lay down naked all that day and all that night' (1 Sam 19.24).

There are damaging effects on people who get drunk on alcohol, such as violence and loss of self-control. The Spirit of God would never lead us into a place where we are not responsible for our actions, or get physically violent. But happiness, singing, laughter, generosity and warm affections are encouraged in Scripture.

Convulsions: most if not all references to do with convulsions have a demonic source. A man with an unclean spirit was silenced by our Lord and the demon was commanded, 'Come out of him!' Mark records that this threw him 'into convulsions, the unclean spirit came out with a loud voice and came out of him' (Mk 1.25–26).

Elsewhere Mark records that someone in the crowd spoke to Jesus about his son who was possessed with a spirit which made him mute. He added, 'Whenever it seizes him it dashes him to the ground and he foams at the mouth and grinds his teeth and stiffens out' (Mk 9.18).

That is why we need to be sure that we are operating in the name of Jesus, in the power of the Holy Spirit and within the Word of God. We also need to ensure that wherever possible we are working in a team and we are not facing these issues on our own. A considerable number of people have been involved in the occult.

Laughter: most evangelicals are a little happier with tears than with laughter, I believe due to a completely wrong concept of reverence. Laughter comes from heaven. 'He who is enthroned in the heavens laughs. . .' (Ps 2.4). He laughs at the wicked as they come to judgment, 'the Lord laughs at him; for he sees his day is coming' (Ps 37.13). Jesus, giving prophetic kingdom teaching, declares 'Blessed are you who weep now, for you shall laugh' (Lk 6.21).

Is it possible our Lord was thinking of Psalm 126, written as a song of thanksgiving after the return from captivity? 'When the Lord brought back those who returned to Zion, we were like those who dream. Then our mouth was filled with laughter, and our tongue with joyful shouting; then they said among the nations, 'The Lord has done great things for them. 'The Lord has done great things for us; we are glad' (Ps 126.1–3).

The Oxford Dictionary describes joy as 'vivid emotion of pleasure, gladness; a thing that causes delight'. The Bible has a great deal to say about joy in a wide range of situations. The apostle Paul was not just joyful in tribulation but 'overflowing with joy in all our afflictions' (2 Cor 7.4). When David wrote a prayer for rescue from his enemies, 'Let them shout for joy and rejoice, who favour my vindication; and let them say continually, "The Lord be magnified" ' (Ps 35.27).

Perhaps most interestingly we have to ask, what is 'joy inexpressible'? (1 Pet 1.8). Indeed the mark of kingdom people is 'righteousness and peace and joy in the Holy Spirit'.

What is laughter? A joy that cannot be communicated with words.

Bodily strength diminished: this phrase was used by Jonathan Edwards but the experience is found in Scripture. Trembling (a partial withdrawing of strength as one might find after an accident or traumatic experience) can happen when there is a divine visitation (Ex 19.16) and angelic visitation (Mt 28.4).

It can also occur when people believe they have heard the voice of God (Mt 17.6), an individual has received a vision (Dan 8.27; 10.11), and could have happened when Peter was having his noonday prayers (Ac 10.10). It certainly happened when Jesus made himself known to what could have been 600 men, a battalion of the Roman cohort (Jn 18.6). Those travelling with Saul to arrest the followers of Christ having seen the light from heaven stood speechless while Saul could see nothing (Ac 9.7–8).

All of this indicates a partial or full withdrawal of physical strength.

Given that Scripture is not given as a proof text for everything, the above is a mere selection of incidents and happenings which are worthy of closer study. I would like to suggest readers do word studies on tears and crying, laughter and joy and the issues raised.

Nevertheless, we need to emphasise the fruit of these phenomena and make room in meetings, public and private, for people to share what Christ has done for them. A trained psychotherapist told a friend of mine that she was 'not yet a Christian' but that she and her colleagues would 'give their right arm' to see in their surgeries what was happening in his church building. She added, 'It takes us two or three years to get people to this point.' She could see it was happening in 20-30 minutes and sometimes even two or three minutes! She concluded that this was very healthy.

While it is inevitable that there will be those who simply look for 'experiences', we should focus on where Christ is at work with or without manifestations.

I am grateful for the research done by Dr Jack Deere, which can be found in his book *Surprised by the Power of the Spirit* (Kingsway).

8

Renewal in the countryside

It is not only town churches which have been experiencing a
new work of the Holy Spirit. When it happened in a village
church in Gloucestershire, it attracted national media interest.
Helen Terry reports from Bream.

In recent years St James' Church, Bream, has developed a
healing and deliverance ministry. People have come forward
during services for individual blessings. This has extended
outwards into the wider community with the vicar and ministry
team making home visits where the blessing of the Holy Spirit
has been prayed for and received.

However, outward manifestations of the Holy Spirit, such as
laughter, weeping, prostrations and deliverance tended to be
limited in their scope, with only one or two church members
being affected at any one time.

In five weeks there has been a massive change of scale with
anything up to 40 being affected simultaneously. There has also
been a mushrooming of media attention. Originally, a story
appeared in the local press. This was then picked up by the
regional press and finally by the nationals. HTV and BBC West
TV camera crews were given permission to film at one small,
subdued midweek service of only 20 church members, seven of
whom 'fell over'. It is interesting how media interest continued.

A *Daily Mail* photographer and reporter arrived at a morning service and were visibly moved by all they witnessed.

It began when the previous vicar, the Rev Philip Rees of London's Ichthus Fellowship, came to visit the present incumbent, Alastair Kendall. He told him of the manifestations of the Holy Spirit that were being experienced in Toronto and churches in London. They decided to hold a meeting at which leaders within St James' and leaders of other churches in the area could hear about the phenomenon, discuss and pray about it.

Many of those attending were blessed by the Holy Spirit. After that the ministry of the Holy Spirit became a regular part of each service. God has worked in different ways in different people. In some people he is working very powerfully and in a very compressed timescale.

A doctor attending one of the services said that God appeared to be dealing in one fell swoop with the old hurts and pains that people had borne for years. He is making a clean sweep which might usually have been expected to take years of 'counselling'.

This does not minimise the anguish that some people are suffering. All the accumulated pain keeps pouring out and they are powerless to prevent it. They have no choice but to cling to God.

There have also been instances of physical healing. For example, over the weeks a woman who had been partially blind has regained three-quarters of her sight. This has been medically confirmed.

Although the Holy Spirit is working in people's lives on both mental and physical levels that does not appear to be the final desired outcome. Instead, they report that they are now bolder in sharing the good news, they hunger and thirst after God and his Word and are desolate when they perceive the depth of their sin.

Within St James' itself the congregation has remained remarkably strong in its resolve to stand together. Naturally, there have been temptations to compare experiences and thereby fall prey to spiritual envy as we think we see God touching others more than ourselves. Therefore we constantly remind ourselves that we are each unique in his creation but equally valuable as members of the body of Christ.

Opinion in the local community has varied from those who malign us for 'turning the church into a circus; it used to be a real church in there, but now they've taken away the pews' to those who are open minded and would be willing to 'give it a go'. At diocesan level, the Bishop of Gloucester is sympathetic with what is taking place.

Is this revival? That seems to be the question on everyone's lips. There are historical precedents which give indications that this could indeed be the case. Prayer for revival has been going on for many years. Could this finally be it? As far as St James' Church is concerned, it is too soon to say.

There has been an increase in the size of congregation but this has tended to be as a result of Christians from other local churches being drawn in as observers rather than transfers. There have also been visitors who are holidaying in the area. So far, the attendance of non-Christians seeking salvation has been small. This could be because, as individuals and as a church, we need to heal ourselves first before we can heal others and spread the good news of Jesus Christ. That will be the acid test. If the outpouring of the Holy Spirit remains in the church, then revival will die in the womb.

For the church, the lasting fruits should be: increased commitment to prayer for revival, commitment to action in the community, increased personal evangelism, and the movement of the Holy Spirit outside the church. As individuals, our behaviour should bear witness to the blessing of the Holy Spirit. '. . . the fruit of the Spirit is love, joy, peace, patience, kindness, goodness, faithfulness, gentleness and self-control' (Gal 5.22).

The Spirit in rural Cornwall

The **Rev Bob Redrup** reports from his parish near Truro.

For us in the parish of Kea, the Holy Spirit's stirring began when one of our members began to hear words from the Lord which were read out to our satellite congregation. In the main, they were calls to holiness and to a deeper realism in our discipleship and worship: we were being urged onwards.

As vicar, I felt the Lord encouraging me during the spring and early summer to offer anointing and prayer to all those who wanted to be closer to Christ and to serve him better. Frequently, as they received the anointing, people were overwhelmed by the Holy Spirit and fell down: some were a little put off by this, others were encouraged. At the heart of it all, though, was a desire to know more of the Lord Jesus, nothing else. Then we heard of similar happenings taking place in London, and one of our young adults came home from Cambridge and reported similar things taking place in her church there.

At a meeting in one of our homes on a Sunday evening, the Holy Spirit was present in a very powerful way. I myself was brought to my knees, and remained there for about half an hour while others experienced tears, laughter, and being unable to remain standing. At a PCC meeting the following week, after essential business was done, we had about an hour and a half of prayer and ministry – and again the presence of the Holy Spirit was felt. There were similar manifestations to those previously experienced and two of our members went home on very unsteady feet.

Then, at a Sunday evening service designed with younger people in mind, there was a time of ministry when, as people prayed for one another, again, the Holy Spirit was present in power. Perhaps the most significant thing here was the desire of children to be prayed for: every child I prayed for wanted to be able to share the love of Christ with his or her friends, and to be a better Christian.

Many were overwhelmed, sometimes almost before prayer had begun. Children then prayed for their friends, and one young lad seemed to spend more time horizontal than vertical as he prayed for those around him.

Manifestations are not important: keeping close to the Lord

Jesus is. We watch and wait to see what fruit comes of this. If, as I believe, this is of God, then our fellowship will be deepened, our love of Christ will be strengthened and our desire to share that love with others will be manifest in our church life. In the meantime, we will welcome all that the Lord does for us, trusting that the glory will be Christ's.

9

Putting it to the test

How do we discern the genuine from the false? The **Rev Dr Mark Stibbe** suggests three theological tests: the test of Christology, the test of character and the test of consequence.

Today there seems to be a rustling of the leaves in the trees – a suggestion of a new movement of God's Spirit in the air. Every day there are reports of dramatic events in many churches. People are breaking into prolonged laughter (which I have experienced myself), weeping and crying out, a sense of conviction and a desire for forgiveness, and so on. Exciting though this is, we must not lose sight of the need to test the spirits. At times like these we do need sound biblical theology to help us to evaluate what we are seeing, hearing and experiencing.

As Richard Lovelace warns, in *Dynamics of Spiritual Life*, we can too quickly rely on 'subjective experience divorced from the objective control of reason and the written Word of God'. So we need theology as well as power, the Word as well as the Spirit. In particular, we need the gift of discernment (1 Cor 12.10). Not everything that is spectacular is necessarily of God. Everything must be weighed and tested using biblical, theological criteria. If we focus only on the exceptional, we may be deceived – and Satan would love to deceive the elect.

First, the test of Christology. Christology – for those

unfamiliar with the word – means 'the study and understanding of the significance of Jesus Christ'. Christology in this sense is extremely relevant in the matter of discernment. Paul clearly teaches us that no one can say that 'Jesus is Lord' except by the Holy Spirit (1 Cor 12.3). The role of the Holy Spirit is to glorify the Lord Jesus. In assessing whether something is a work of the Holy Spirit, we therefore need to ask, 'Does it exalt the Lord Jesus?'

Jonathan Edwards, in *The Distinguishing Marks of a Work of the Spirit of God* (1741), also made Christology the first criterion for discernment when the 'great and general awakening' spread throughout New England. The test of Christology is essential.

The second criterion is that of character. As is well known, Paul places his two major discussions of the spiritual gifts (1 Cor 12 and 14) before and after a great eulogy of love (1 Cor 13). This was no doubt because many of the Corinthian charismatics were becoming proud of their spiritual gifts and were starting to cause division in the church. To counter this, Paul speaks of love as the great test of authentic Christian spirituality. He gives priority to the fruit rather than the gifts: to character rather than charisma.

This is also helpful. When assessing various phenomena, we need to ask, 'Does this work produce a new expression of *agape* (self-giving love) in a fellowship? Does it manifest the primary fruit of the Spirit that is 'love'? Are walls of prejudice, division and unforgiveness coming down as a result of these events?'

Third is the test of consequence. Jonathan Edwards warned his contemporaries that they should not be too swayed by immediate demonstrations of power. What counts is what comes afterwards – the consequences. He urged the churches to enquire: what fruit has been produced? Is there a new zeal for attacking the kingdom of darkness in all its manifestations? Does this work honour Scripture? Does it promote sound doctrine? Does it result in a new passion for God? As Jesus said, 'Every tree that does not bear good fruit is cut down and thrown into the fire. By their fruit you will recognise them' (Mt 7.19–20).

As far as the test of Christology is concerned, people seem to be discovering a new intimacy in their relationship with the Lord Jesus Christ. A Baptist pastor who has been involved with the events at the Vineyard church in Toronto reports a renewing of commitment and spiritual vision and a rekindled passion for Jesus and for the work of the kingdom.

As far as the test of character is concerned (love), there are also some encouraging signs. In Toronto the new wave of blessing is embracing people of every denomination. As Eleanor Mumford wrote, 'Jesus is breaking down the barriers of his church because he is coming for a bride and he wants his bride to be one.' Certainly a new spirit of love seems to be emerging.

As far as the test of consequence is concerned, it is encouraging how various leaders are stressing the need to look to the future. 'It is to the fruit that we look rather than the signs,' writes Sandy Millar. Already there are signs of fruitfulness. The events of these last few months are clearly leading to changed lives. One Baptist minister has reported that 'rededications are numerous, conversions are being witnessed'. Examining the current dramatic events under these criteria, we must conclude that this is a work of the Holy Spirit.

My own experience bears this out. I had a profound experience of refreshment at Holy Trinity, Brompton, which produced, among other things, a great release of joy. This has now broken out in our church in Sheffield as well.

Is this revival? That, of course, depends upon your definition of revival. My own feeling is that it is too early to give that kind of label to the current work of the Spirit. I believe that this present movement of God is about the restoration of first love. God is renewing in many weary and battle-worn Christians the joy of their salvation. He is renewing that sense of God's 'nearness to me and my dearness to him', to quote Jonathan Edwards' wife. That in itself is a great and marvellous thing. Alleluia!

Those who feel left out

Was something wrong? Was something unconfessed? Had God missed him out? The man went home disappointed. From her own experience **Jane Grayshon** offers a possible explanation.

In the wave of excitement following the 'Toronto blessing' coming to Britain, it seems a dampener to ask, 'What about those who feel left out?' Some Christians earnestly seek God's blessing and do not see it. I am not referring here to those who deliberately hang back out of derision or even fear. Nor am I talking about those who turn their back on blessing because they prefer the familiar habit of hugging their hurts.

Take the scene at a large meeting in west London for example. This was at a mid-week meeting, when the Holy Spirit was pouring his gifts extravagantly all around. There was laughter, rest and refreshment to the soul, singing in tongues, even physical healing for one friend who arrived in her wheelchair and departed pushing it in front of her.

In one part of the church a man was being prayed with, prayed for, prayed over. As the prayer continued and nothing seemed to happen to him, his face visibly changed from hope and eager anticipation to an earnest intensity. He wanted a sign of God's touch; he wanted to share in whatever was available from God. Gradually his expression became more puzzled. He was neither laughing nor crying; neither dancing nor resting peacefully.

The ministry team member praying for him became increasingly authoritative. 'More of you, Lord!' were the words. But there was nothing visible. No memorable touch from God. It was evident that God was not doing as he was asked.

An hour later that man went home disappointed. He had seen God draw tangibly close to others, but not to him. He no doubt identified closely with those left unhealed by the pool at Bethesda; or with the many people in Capernaum left looking for Jesus while he himself withdrew saying, 'Let's go elsewhere' (Mk 1.38).

It's hard. Certainly it's easier to quote quickly some reason as to why God might withhold his blessing, than to acknowledge that there is a time to be silent as well as a time to speak.

Perhaps God did answer the prayer for 'more of him'. I wondered if he wanted to show that we can receive more of him as deeply in silent communion with him as we can in laughter or other special signs. Silent communion should not be despised, any more than drunk-looking laughter. Or perhaps we should ask ourselves, What exactly is our hope, our longing, as we wait on him? Is our hope for God alone? Or is it – if we are honest – for refreshment and joy?

We yearn for God, and as humans we want to see him touch us. We want a sign of his visitation. Sometimes, it is in not receiving the joy or the refreshment that we are caused to realise that we have confused the manifestation of God's presence with God himself.

God's Spirit is with us, even when we are unaware of him. God does bless us, even when our lives do not look like it. We can see this in Abram. God had specifically promised, 'I will bless you,' but it was Lot, not Abram, who got to live in the lush land of Jordan. When Abram realised that he had missed out on a land so nice-looking that it was 'like the garden of the Lord', he must have wondered whether God's promised 'blessings' had been thwarted. Yet it was in the barren-looking land that Abram received the richest blessings. He had apparently missed out on the goodies, but God did bless him.

While I was seriously ill, my husband Matthew and I prayed – and others prayed with me, for me, over me – begging for an end to the intolerable level of suffering. What God gave was blessing indeed. But it was very different from physical healing which is quickly recognised as 'blessing'. Somehow, and I cannot pinpoint how, God revealed his heart. Through the suffering, he invited me to share his brokenness with him. It lasted for 15 years. I can only describe it as holy ground. His gift was given through pain; because of pain.

At this point one gets caught in the eternal question, 'But how can God allow . . .', to which the answer is that I don't know. What I do know is that he gave gifts, and blessing, and refreshment where they were least expected. And I know that he has not confined all this to me.

There are some who measure the activity of God by visible signs and wonders. But I believe that to do so is to put blinkers on, and blind ourselves to the unseen grace at work within. I wonder if sometimes we seek and we find, yet we do not see. God's work is so different from what we expect. It is possible for us not even to recognise him, never mind appreciate him.

A different question is how much we should listen to those offended by the more demonstrative meetings. It seems to be the public expression of the love-relationship with God which is hard to accept. We expect a man and woman to express their love privately. Should we be less private in the giving and receiving of love with God when the body is as involved as during this movement of the Holy Spirit?

One cannot be altogether surprised that some, especially visitors or onlookers, have found the spectacle to be distasteful. We cannot deny that in the display of such raw excitement, some people reach a distinct spiritual 'high'. Well, some do, some don't. Probably the worst bit for those who don't is they feel they are simply missing out on the fun.

The truth is that it is possible to seek the fun for its own sake. We are human. Of course we know there can be full expression of love without sparks flying but . . . it seems unfair to do the duty without having the fun too.

It is lovely, most lovely, when God seems to invite spirit and emotions to join together, the one unleashing the other in tears or in laughter which makes our very soul soar. But we must challenge one another, and challenge ourselves, with the call to seek God first. It is not for our own pleasure that we respond to him, but for his sake. For his glory.

Habakkuk said,

> Though the fig tree does not bud and there are no grapes on the vines, though the olive crop fails and the fields produce no food, though there are no sheep in the pen and no cattle in the stalls, yet I will rejoice in the Lord, I will be joyful in God my Saviour.
> (Hab 3.17,18)

These words might have cheered the man who felt left out. Habakkuk was determined that, even with no sign at all of God's blessing, he would still rejoice. He would let nothing stem his determination to be joyful in God himself . . . no matter what happened. Or didn't happen.

II
Sunderland revisited

Night after night, week after week, between 300 and 700 people have gathered in the excitement of renewal, report **Andy and Jane Fitz-Gibbon.** Each night there are powerful demonstrations of the Spirit of God as people receive anew the anointing from God. Hearts are renewed, spirits are refreshed, people fall down, laugh, cry, groan, shout.

But this is not Toronto, nor Argentina, nor even London. It is the north-east coastal town of Sunderland, birthplace of Pentecostalism in the British Isles.

In 1907 the Holy Spirit was poured out upon the Church of All Saints, Monkwearmouth, Sunderland. Alexander Boddy, vicar of the church, was radically changed and the torch of Spirit baptism was lit and carried throughout the UK, Europe and beyond. Between September 1907 and April 1908 it was said that over 500 people received the baptism in the Spirit in the parish hall of All Saints. Phenomena associated with revival were seen in abundance. The *Sunderland Echo* in September 1907 reported fainting, laughter and 'intense excitement'. So profound was God's work at Sunderland that T B Barrett (an English pastor, transplanted to Norway and part of the renewal at Sunderland in September and October 1907) made a journal entry which read, 'The eyes of all the religious millions of Great Britain are now fixed upon Sunderland.'

But this is not 1907. In 1994 God began to re-dig the well in

Sunderland. He has revisited a place of former blessing. Those of us associated with the renewal have been astounded at the intensity, the prolonged nature and vitality of this move of God.

The place of God's present visitation is Sunderland Christian Centre (SCC), a beautiful new building. It comfortably seats 600, though, when John and Carol Arnott visited in October 1994, 1,200 were packed in. It is situated in the midst of one of the roughest parts of north-east England. The building is surrounded by a 10-foot perimeter fence. All glass in the building is brick-proof polycarbonate. Each night of the renewal meetings, cars of the participants are guarded by security guards, contracted from a local security firm.

At the time of writing, for a period of 22 weeks every night (except Monday) people have gathered from all over the north and beyond.

In north-east England we had heard rumours of a new outpouring early in summer 1994. Anne Watson had visited Heaton Baptist Church, Newcastle, in the May and had shared her experiences of a new and transmittable blessing. However, it was not until August that a number of leaders from the north-east made their way to Toronto to see for themselves.

Ken and Lois Gott, senior pastors at SCC, had founded the church eight years ago. In 1992 they moved to the new building thanks to the generosity and sacrificial giving of the people. Ken admits however that by summer 1994 he was spiritually dried up. His ministry had been successful in all outward ways, but inside he had a longing to know God in a deeper way. He visited Holy Trinity, Brompton, in August with four other Pentecostal leaders and was deeply humbled by the sense of God among, of all people, Anglicans! Stereotypes were shattered as Ken and the other Pentecostalists received a new baptism in the Spirit at the hands of Bishop David Pytches.

The change was so profound in Ken that the members at SCC took up an offering and sent Ken, Lois and their youth leader for a week in Toronto. Like most of us who have made the same pilgrimage, they were profoundly touched, 'soaking' in God for a week, never to be the same again.

On the return flight the Gotts made a decision not to tell the church about the phenomena. Ken reflects, 'We wanted to have a visitation, not an imitation.' The outcome exceeded all their expectations.

On their return, the Holy Spirit landed on SCC! In a similar fashion to the beginnings at Airport Vineyard, the church met nightly, thinking the experience would last for a few nights. After two weeks of nightly meetings without a break, it seems the renewal 'kicked into another gear'. Without advertisement, word began to extend across the region. People started to come to SCC from a spread of 70 miles. Numbers attending in the third week grew to 600 a night. The meetings begin at 7.30pm (6.30pm Sundays) and ministry usually continues to about 11.00pm, though there have been occasions when the ministry team are still praying into the early hours of the morning.

People come from all denominations, with the biggest spread possible. Catholics lie on the carpet next to the Plymouth Brethren. Anglican priests have fallen, shaken, and jerked along with the Baptists. In the most amazing way walls have come down between people. Brothers and sisters long separated have found a new love and respect for one another. In one meeting at opposite sides of the room sat two pastors who were divided from each other through a painful church spilt. They both came forward to testify to God's renewed love and found reconciliation with each other. Their churches decided to hold a meeting in their city together.

Each night testimonies are given to God's changing people's hearts and lives. One woman testified a month and a half after her first visit that 'God has done for me in six weeks what counsellors have tried to do for 10 years', so deep was the change in her life. Teenagers have been given new boldness in testifying of their faith to their friends. Children as young as seven or eight are seeing amazing visions and publicly giving testimony that they know God is with them. There have been dramatic physical healings and a great increase in the release of prophecy.

Early in the renewal it was decided to open out the meetings to all those whom God was touching. There is nothing 'exclusive' or denominational about the renewal. Each night there is a ministry team composed of members of different churches throughout the region. Leading and preaching is done by a team of pastors and others who have been touched by the refreshing. The renewal meetings have become a melting-pot of God's people in the north-east. We are learning to love each other and new and deep friendships have been made.

Among those who have come have been pastors and their spouses needing a fresh touch from God. Most have been spiritually dry, some even on the point of resigning from the ministry before they came to Sunderland. Many of these have testified to a renewed vision, a new sense of direction and a new empowering and anointing. Having been met powerfully, they have returned home and God has transformed their churches. Indeed, dozens of churches in the north-east are now enjoying the refreshing. One of the fruits of the renewal is a monthly leaders' meeting where around 250 from all denominations gather to share in what God is doing.

Lois Gott says that at SCC now there are two works. 'One is the local church, which was here before the refreshing. The other is the renewal centre, which is a well for people to drink from every night.'

To keep pace with the renewal, and to provide adequate care for the local church, Ken and Lois have been set apart to work full-time in the refreshing, giving them a wider brief than the local church. Jim and Lesley Beattie moved into the role of pastors to care for the local church.

Needless to say, the effect on the church itself has been profound. Membership doubled in 1994, to just over 400. There have been many commitments to Christ during the renewal meetings. Exact numbers are difficult to ascertain as people come from a wide geographical spread. Coach-loads have come from Preston, Carlisle, Hull and other places. However, since the renewal started, there have been over 25 commitments to

Christ which have been 'processed' at SCC; that is, people who have made a commitment, been discipled and are now active in the local fellowship.

Some of those commitments have been dramatic and profound. One man, who had a criminal past, was brought to the meetings by his girlfriend. Halfway through the meeting he ran out, unable to cope with what was happening. A few days later he was back, gave his life to Christ and received the Holy Spirit in a powerful and dramatic way. The effect was life-changing. This man has, since his conversion, been used to lead others to Christ and is a shining testimony to the grace of God.

Like many in other parts of the country, we have been asking God where the next step lies. We believe we are in a period of preparation for a great ingathering of new believers. In God's goodness we will integrate them into churches newly alive with the power and love of God. We are aware that we can only take people into places we have been ourselves. As people find Christ, we believe that they will be led into a passionate Christianity which has a new love affair with the Lord Jesus Christ.

In January 1995 the renewal at Sunderland moved to two meetings a day with a daily prayer meeting in the afternoon. Like many around the country, we are praying that the renewal will lead on to revival, with a harvest of many finding Christ.

12

Making sense of the Spirit's move

God is pouring out his Spirit in a fresh – and for most of us
unprecedented – way. **Terry Virgo** sees Acts 10 and 11 as very
instructive as we seek to understand the experiences now
occurring around the world.

I have recently found myself arrested by the account of Peter
and Cornelius, recorded in Acts 10. You probably recall the
story. After a remarkable series of supernatural events, Peter
preaches the gospel to Cornelius and his household, who
experience a dramatic outpouring of the Holy Spirit.

The sheer number of spiritual phenomena – angelic
visitations, a trance, a vision, God's audible voice, and an
outbreak of speaking in tongues – makes the story noteworthy.
The fact that this outpouring occurred among Gentiles is
especially notable. It forced the Jewish believers to revisit some
deeply-held (and false) assumptions about God.

Acts 10 and 11 mark a turning point in the history of the
church. As God overflowed the banks of their previous
experience, they began to understand that the frontiers of their
calling far exceeded the limitations they had set.

The outpouring in Cornelius' household did not originate with
a strategy meeting among the apostles. Peter himself was initially
unwilling. The other apostles were questioning and critical. This
was God's initiative, and it took the apostles by surprise.

We see such surprises throughout history. The church has not grown in steady, predictable increments over the centuries. You cannot project a graph into the future and say, 'Well, we're here now, so we'll be there ultimately.' Church history can only be understood in the context of revivals.

Ian Murray says in his book, *The Puritan Hope*, that the Puritans held that 'the kingdom of Christ would spread in triumph through powerful operations of the Holy Spirit poured out upon the church in revivals.' Church history has always had these flood times, supernatural surges when God suddenly takes the field again, breaking in and altering history.

In Acts 10 we have such an occasion. The church was making excellent progress. Then the God of glory said, 'It's time for the next phase, the great Gentile breakout.' The initiative came from heaven. Often a new move of the Spirit clashes with previous experience. In Jerusalem, the apostles could not understand why Peter had violated tradition and ministered among Gentiles. Because they remained flexible and open to the Spirit, they were able to adapt to this fresh flow from God. Tragically, the church has often refused to adapt.

At many junctures God has blown a fresh breath into the church through men like John Wesley or William Booth, yet they have been rejected and forced out of the mainstream. I pray this current move of the Spirit won't lead to another splintering. If we will learn to be flexible when God breathes, we can hold together.

As I read through Acts 10, I am amazed at all that Peter and Cornelius experienced. We read of an angel, a trance, a vision — not just a vague, mystical sense, but heaven invading Peter's life – an audible voice, and the Spirit leading and falling on people so that they are overwhelmed. All in one chapter! Not quite our typical level of church life, but this is all biblical. How much we need to rediscover the Spirit's ability to communicate to us directly.

Researchers estimate the world population will double by the year 2020. A 'bookish' religion would be out of reach for so many of them. But even the most illiterate peasant understands when the Spirit moves in power.

Tragically, our modern Western world has great difficulty with anything supernatural. So does the church at large, for that matter. But we must insist that the supernatural is part of the church's inheritance – even if, like Peter, we find ourselves 'greatly perplexed in mind' regarding the Spirit's manifestations (Ac 16.17 NAS).

When I was at Bible college in the 1960s, I arranged for Arthur Wallis to come as a visiting speaker. He spoke on revival and referred to the breath-taking miracles that were taking place at that time in Indonesia. It was a marvellous evening. Yet the next day I was grieved to hear the faculty expressing concern about having 'such speakers'.

The following evening I was at Westminster Chapel, where Dr Martyn Lloyd-Jones was teaching from Acts 8. He was at his glorious best as he preached on Philip in Samaria and the gospel and signs and wonders. I drank it in. Here was this greatly respected theologian saying things so similar to what I had heard the evening before.

Afterwards I had a chance to speak to him, and related some of what Arthur Wallis had shared. 'You're preaching what I believe in,' I said, 'yet we're not seeing many signs and wonders. I just believe it is part of what God has for us.' I will never forget his response. 'The greatest sin of the evangelical church,' he said 'is that we want to put God in a little box and tell him what he is permitted to do and what he's not permitted to do.'

We must overcome the temptation to prescribe what God can and cannot do. It's his church. We must be open to him when he moves and breaks in rather than confining him to our own limited experience. 'God is a God who speaks to us not only through words, but by actions. It has always been so: at the Red Sea, at Jericho's walls, at the banks of the River Jordan.

Again and again we have seen the majesty and might of God displayed through his actions. Our God not only speaks to us –

he acts. When we witness his actions, we need to employ Scripture's teachings to make sure our understanding is accurate. This is essential. But I feel one of the things God is saying to us is, 'Listen. Listen to know me more personally. Listen to know me more intimately, and not only through your study. Don't merely be a cerebral people.' Nevertheless, as I have tasted of these recent experiences, I find I am reading theology more avidly than ever before.

Acts 10 contains some amazing incidents many believers and unbelievers alike would find almost impossible to understand. 'An angel came to you? You heard a voice? People interrupted your sermon by responding to the Holy Spirit? This is really strange.'

Here in the West we have lagged behind in our experience of the Holy Spirit. We cannot reduce church merely to under-standing certain doctrines or performing good works. The church is a supernatural creation. And a supernatural people should be at home in the supernatural dimension.

It was God who initiated the events in Cornelius' household, and it is God who has initiated this current season of refreshing. He refuses to be put in a box. He is giving churches around the world first-hand encounters with a power they have studied but never experienced. yet he expects us to employ biblical knowledge to conserve and benefit from this outpouring.

Look at how Peter reported to the elders in Jerusalem. Rather than giving them a mystical description of the experience, he 'proceeded to explain to them in orderly sequence' what had occurred (Ac 11.4 NAS). The New International Version says he 'explained everything to them precisely as it had happened'. The phrasing reminds me of the introduction to Luke's Gospel: 'Since I myself have carefully investigated everything from the beginning, it seemed good also to me to write an orderly account for you, most excellent Theophilus, so that you may know the certainty of the things you have been taught' (Lk 1.3–4). Of course Luke goes on to relate strange and wonderful events – angelic choirs and messengers, a virgin and old woman conceiving, a man struck dumb, and so on. Yet having done his research, he sets it out in an orderly way for others to see.

Moving into the supernatural does not mean you kiss your brain goodbye and wait to see where you wind up. It's not like that. It may be amazing, outside our normal realm, but we should be able to articulate from Scripture the precedent and purpose for what's happening.

On the day of Pentecost, in the midst of that glorious first outpouring, Peter was able to stand and explain. 'This is what was spoken by the prophet Joel' (Ac 2.16). For those who have personally experienced recent manifestations, as strange and indescribable as they may seem, it is very important that we love others enough to explain as best we can what's happening.

This type of outbreak invariably raises huge questions. It's not helpful to say, 'Well, it's too wonderful to communicate. You just need to experience it, then you'll know.' Peter explained very carefully. We owe it to our brothers and sisters to explain any new experience in the Holy Spirit as fully as possible.

News of Peter's experience with Cornelius reached Jerusalem before he did (Ac 11.1). This kind of news always travels fast. There is nothing wrong with testing a new direction to make sure it is from God. As we encounter new things, we must respect those who have questions and give them space to enquire and research Scripture. Sometimes we see God doing something new, something fresh, but there are things around it which we find unacceptable.

In this present move of the Spirit, I have attended meetings where I was extremely blessed, but witnessed and heard things I felt were questionable. In fact, I have never seen so many strange things in all my life! I am grateful that early on in this outpouring I saw supernatural experiences lead to dramatically changed lives.

Marriages have been restored in our church, the recalcitrant have been humbled, and the timid have begun witnessing boldly. Half-hearted attenders have become zealots for God.

When I saw changes like these taking place – and because of the Spirit's work they occurred in a matter of moments rather than months – that convinced me far more than any number of people falling down.

I have seen a mixture here and there, and have winced at certain doctrinal references. In a move of this magnitude there are bound to be some mistakes. But I have resolved to lay hold of what is from God. Despite those things that may be unacceptable, look at all that is acceptable. Look at what God is doing!

If we will remain committed to biblical truth, while opening ourselves up to this fresh move, I am convinced that God will bring together truth and Spirit and help us build something strong for his glory.

If ever a sad, sin-sick society needed an outpouring of God's holy presence and power, it's ours. All we need to know is, 'is it you, Lord?' With all my heart I am convinced the answer is yes.

Similar phenomena preceded the revival in Argentina, a country that has seen hundreds of thousands saved in the last decade. I earnestly believe this season of refreshing is the prelude to a great international revival. The banquet has been spread. The wine is poured out. It's time to come and receive.

13

'Toronto' for your children?

John and Christine Leach's book *And for Your Children*, on leading children in the Spirit's way, aroused considerable comment. The Leach family have had a further experience of the Holy Spirit, which prompted these observations.

We do need to say first that we firmly believe that the present movement generally known as the Toronto blessing, is, in fact, a genuine move of the Spirit of God. It does seem to be about awakening and refreshing the church: whether or not it leads on to full-scale revival will depend to a large extent on how we in the churches handle it. Keeping it on the twin tracks of biblical truth and honour to Jesus should keep it running, but the potential we have to distort and therefore stop the work of God is staggering, as history tells us so eloquently.

But what about children? For us the experience began there. The Sunday evening when we just happened to be in London and ended up at Holy Trinity, Brompton, was the first time we had heard of this new wave of blessing. But it was our Steve, aged 12, who was touched the most strongly, and has catalysed its coming to our church and city. He lay on the floor writhing and laughing for about 20 minutes while the rest of us were just gently wobbling.

Since then we have seen an increasing degree of the Spirit's work at our own church, but more significantly in the church in

Coventry, as many of us meet together rather than apart on one Sunday evening each month. On each occasion there have been significant numbers of children and teenagers present and they have been involved up to the hilt.

It is significant that, as our children have seen and heard bizarre sights and sounds, have watched people crash to the floor, have witnessed weeping and sobbing, and have heard all sorts of noises, there has not been a hint of fear. They have looked on in vague bemusement, or have found it hilarious fun, or have joined those laughing on the floor. But they have not wanted to run or escape in the way that many adults have.

The atmosphere seems to have been one where they felt at home. We find it one of the most convincing arguments for this to be a move of God rather than a satanic deception or just human enthusiasm. So, if you are a terrified or even slightly apprehensive adult, don't be afraid to expose your children to occasions when you know God will come in these kinds of ways. The only thing which will make them afraid is your fear, not the manifestations themselves.

We need to be very careful that we don't remove children from possible blessing because we can't cope with it. Let's be painfully honest as well: don't let's tell people we are staying away because our children might get scared when really the issue is our own fear.

As mentioned, we have seen children on the receiving end of God's blessing. The external manifestations seem to be similar to those among adults: laughing or crying, falling over, shaking or writhing. What really counts, however, is the fruit, and that's more of a long-term process. The general consensus among those who have received from God during this wave is that over a period they have found themselves more in love with Jesus, talking to him more in prayer, reading about him more in the Bible, and talking about him more to others.

We would expect the same among our children. In fact comments have included, 'I feel much more happy all the time' (no bad thing); 'I think about Jesus much more than I did before' (even better); and 'I've got much more courage in telling my friends I'm a Christian.' Even more significant is the widely expressed feeling that those who felt themselves to be only marginally useful to God can now see that he really values, loves and uses them. There is a deeper awareness of Jesus' love for them, a new confidence and spring in the steps of their walk with the Lord, and a vastly increased hunger for the Spirit.

The really exciting part about this move of the Spirit is the way in which we have seen children ministering to others. It has always been our desire to involve children in ministry. We have seen it in the context of our children's ministry to quite a degree, but we have been less successful in all-age contexts. Not any more. The reason, we believe, is that nowadays it's so easy and so much fun. They can't keep their hands off people, and when they pray they see the same things they see when grown-ups pray. What we have been struggling to see for 10 years or more, we are seeing week after week, and it's all so quick and so powerful. These are heady days for all of us, but for our children they are just tremendous fun.

Our aim as adults, therefore, is to do two things. First, we want to encourage them all we can to be involved. As well as helping them practically to minister, we want to work on a changed attitude. This means that we are just as open and expectant to receive when we open our eyes and see a child praying for us as we would be for an adult. We will feed back to them everything good we can possibly think of, and gently and lovingly correct anything unhelpful in the way they prayed.

Second, we need to help them to grow up in their understanding of what is going on: to come to a profound understanding of the sovereign work of God, which it is our privilege to be a part of for a while. We find it distasteful to think of ourselves as having 'done it': we push such self-glorifying feelings quickly from our minds and offer thanks instead to God. Perhaps there are ways in which we can both learn from and teach our children; a very biblical pattern.

We can learn from their sense of fun and adventure. We

recently visited a local church which has so far not seen any 'Toronto' manifestations. It is hidebound with all sorts of problems and traditions and personalities from the past which keep the congregation in terrified submission, and which God is only slowly beginning to break down. Discussing 'Toronto' with us, the vicar's wife exclaimed wistfully, 'It would really do our people good to laugh in church.' Children are having fun in the church in ways which just wouldn't have been their experience a few months ago. It will be to our loss if we stay so serious and po-faced about it all that we miss something of the party which God is giving us at the moment. We need to make sure, however, that our fun is filled with awe and gratitude, and that the focus remains on Jesus. We can help them with that bit.

No doubt the debate will go on over whether or not 'Toronto' is a 'blessing', and whether or not we should let our youngsters within a hundred miles of it. Initial reactions to our book *And for Your Children* have not so far been surprising: those who are quite happy with the supernatural work of the Spirit have welcomed know-how on including children, while those terrified of anything to do with him (and of course those terrified of their own emotions) have regarded it as the paperback from hell. Even the spell-checker on the computer wanted to change 'Brompton' to 'brimstone'!

It all depends on your starting point. But if God is indeed refreshing and renewing his church – and we firmly believe he is – we want our children refreshed and renewed too.

And for Your Children is published by Monarch.

14

The Spirit and evangelism

On the evening before this interview with **Nicky Gumbel** there
had been an Alpha supper at Holy Trinity, Brompton. The nave
now has flexible seating instead of pews and it had been
arranged to accommodate 650 people at the tables. In fact, over
1,100 people had accepted invitations so the event was spread
over two evenings. Many people are won for Christ through the
Alpha courses, then they invite their friends to come to the next
supper and these friends are in turn invited to the next course.
The number of Christians keeps multiplying. The Alpha method
began at Holy Trinity, Brompton, but has spread to 1,000
churches throughout the country, with leaders being trained
through Alpha conferences.

Nicky Gumbel believes it is no coincidence that the present
movement of the Holy Spirit has come at the same time as the
explosion of the Alpha courses. . .

I think the two go together. If you run an Alpha course –
certainly the way we run it here and encourage other
churches to run it – there will be an opportunity for people to
experience the Holy Spirit during the course, in whatever way
is applicable to that particular church. That inevitably leads to
renewal. Similarly, if a church has been powerfully touched by
the Spirit of God, 'you will be my witnesses', as Jesus said.
This need not be through the Alpha course, it may be through
another way, but many churches are finding that the Alpha
course is an ideal model for them to use for evangelism.

We are now nearly a year on from when the Holy Spirit fell

with power on our staff meeting at Holy Trinity, Brompton. The power that we saw on that first occasion has in no way lessened. Indeed, if anything it has increased. That has been true of people's experiences, both here and as they have gone out in teams to various parts of the country. Two people have just reported back after a visit to a prison, where they saw the most wonderful outpouring of the Spirit. At all the Alpha conferences we have had the same experience.

Everybody is resisting using the term 'revival', but it depends how revival is being defined. One definition is 'bringing new life'. We are certainly seeing new life coming into the church and people outside the church being affected. Our experience of the Alpha courses here, and the reports I get back from the courses round the country, is that they are seeing people coming to faith in Christ, being filled with the Spirit, getting excited about Jesus and telling their friends. More and more people are getting converted.

If you think in terms of 1,000 courses and an average of 20–30 people coming into that experience and telling their friends and getting them onto a course, and that is happening three times a year, then a great many people are involved. My prayer is that not just 1,000 but maybe several thousand churches run Alpha courses in the future. I am not saying that Alpha is the only way, there are other methods being used. Altogether, hundreds of thousands of people outside the church could be affected.

God is just pouring out his love on people of all ages, from children to the very elderly. The children respond very naturally. They are not fazed by it, nor frightened at all. A woman in her seventies, who has been coming to the church here for at least 40 years, is part of the more traditional, old Holy Trinity congregation that was here before any of the things that we have been seeing. She has been having a wonderful time, praying for people and seeing the Spirit of God come upon them. There is another woman in the congregation who has prayed for 50 years to see such a spiritual renewal. You should see her face now. She is so alive, and so excited at seeing her prayers being answered.

I believe it is important always to keep in view the supreme goal, which is that God's name is honoured and his kingdom comes. That must mean keeping evangelism to the fore. I think that is what people are wanting to do. There is a great desire to go out with the message and to preach the gospel and see people's lives changed. That is exciting.

The comment has been made that there has generally been little emphasis on repentance, but we have been seeing many, many instances of repentance. People are leaving behind the old life because they have seen something better. We have seen a lot of weeping over past sins. One woman wept for an hour over an abortion she had had 18 years previously. We have seen people lying on the floor crying out, 'I repent of my sins, I repent of my sins.' It is a wonderful kind of repentance. It's like the repentance of the prodigal son: he turned round, changed his mind and his father welcomed him with open arms. There was joy and celebration. That's what we are seeing here.

Repentance is very positive, as it is in the New Testament. People are changing their lifestyle. When they have experienced God they don't want to lose that new relationship so inevitably that means changes in their lives.

The church needs to pray, and there are two topics that I feel particularly strongly about. First, we need to unite. We need to encourage one another, encourage whatever God is doing in different places, not try to put our experience onto any other church. Let us be thrilled by what God is doing, wherever he is doing it. There has been some comment which is not altogether helpful to unity. Let us drop that and get on. It is wonderful that the movement of the Spirit will always bring churches together. He is doing that right across the denominations and within the traditions.

Locally we have always worked with all the denominations, and all the Alpha conferences go right across the board. We are seeing Roman Catholics coming now, as well as Anglicans, Methodists, Baptists, United Reformed, Pentecostals and members of new churches. Nobody is suspicious of anybody else. Everyone is working together and I believe that is what the Spirit achieves. The Spirit brings unity to the church. People are no longer 'labelling' themselves or others. I long for the day when we drop all these labels and just regard ourselves as Christians with a commission from Jesus Christ. A disunited church, squabbling and criticising, makes it very hard for the world to believe.

A second great concern in prayer should be evangelism. If the church just gets caught up with itself, that is very sad. Personally, I don't see any signs of that. We are seeing, thankfully, a new concentration on evangelism. As on the day of Pentecost. when people were filled with the Holy Spirit, they want to spread the message. That is surely a mark of the work of the Spirit.

I am not consciously aware of having referred to this movement of the Spirit as the Toronto blessing. It may be a handy piece of shorthand but this work of the Holy Spirit seems to be world-wide and it is the Lord's blessing. We are all very grateful to the Airport Vineyard church in Toronto but even John Arnott, the senior pastor there, has said that he would not refer to it as the Toronto blessing.

People have been trying to trace human roots for it, but Jesus said, 'By their fruits you will know them'. I think we should look at the fruit. The fruit is the test, but there are people wanting to make the roots the test. I have not had the opportunity of meeting any of the people who are supposed to be the roots. We are praying not for the spirit of 'X' to fill people but for the Holy Spirit to fill them. I think it is irrelevant that so-and-so is linked with so-and-so, who once met so and so, who was into something that wasn't very good. Actually we must stop judging one another.

We are not doing anything differently from the way we have done it before. The only difference is that we are seeing people having more powerful experiences of God. God is sovereignly choosing to pour out his love on the church and on individuals. We are simply praying for God's Spirit to come. Jesus said,

'How much more will your Father in heaven give the Holy Spirit to all who ask it?' That is all we are doing. We are asking him to give the Holy Spirit: more of his Spirit to people. And we are seeing him do it. Thanks be to God for his indescribable gift!

15

On the crest of the Spirit's wave

Gerald Coates gives a personal comment on the present movement of the Spirit and relates his experiences of how lives are being changed and a new dynamic for evangelism is emerging.

I was raised just outside London, among a group of fairly strict Christians – the Plymouth Brethren. We expressed neither fun-filled joy, nor tearful remorse or sadness. We were a well intentioned, sincere group but with not an emotion on the horizon.

For me the Christian life was well ordered, punctual, practical, safe, certain and without risk. Of course it had its good points, particularly as we observe the apparent chaos of life today. But as I studied the life, behaviour, teaching and outlook of Christianity's founder, another picture emerged. It was one of informality, humour, a risky faith that was real and gutsy. It was not nearly so neatly ordered.

Jesus Christ came to forgive wrongdoers, heal sick souls and bodies and mend relationships. In fact he came to bring non-violent change to the entire planet. So when he started his mission, his 'journey with a purpose' as someone called it, he would start it with a miracle. What astounding, attention-grabbing miracle would set his three-year ministry in motion?

Lightning from heaven? The bad guys frizzled to ashes? The Romans visited by armies of angels and booted out of the Promised Land? No, not quite. He turned umpteen gallons of water into a first-class wine. Hmm, this is different.

The very presence of Jesus proclaimed to both the religious and the irreligious that it was party time. Partying is not yet the nation's image of the church. Numerical decline has slowed down: one million in the 70s, half a million in the 80s, a quarter in the 90s. The church is still seen as a serious, ageing, sober bunch of nice folk.

Over the last few months, however, there have been some extraordinary occurrences. Informality, laughter and tears and people lying on the floor are not new to Pentecostals and charismatics. But this was different. It was more intense. It is the fastest thing that has spread throughout the church in my lifetime.

People claim to have a much closer awareness of Christ, find it necessary to confess things they have done wrong in the past and apologise to others for doing wrong. Many testify to an increased appetite for prayer, reading the Scriptures and sharing their faith in a sensitive way.

Many wise Christian leaders, who have seen or read about similar things in the Scripture or in contemporary revival, have said that these are 'times of refreshing in the presence of the Lord' (Ac 3.19).

Throughout the spring of 1994 I was engaged in considerable travels. I spoke in Orebro, Sweden; Geneva; Dublin; Frankfurt, and at John Mumford's South-west London Vineyard. In all those places we saw crying, confession of fears and wrongdoing, laughter and people who after prayer would lie on the floor for up to an hour. It was impressive. But not nearly as impressive as what Eleanor Mumford was experiencing in Toronto over the same weekend that I was at the South-west London Vineyard. When she returned she explained to her own church and to Holy Trinity, Brompton, what she had seen, and her own experience. After a short time of silence, the same laughter, tears, shaking and falling to the floor occurred (see chapter 2). In no time the national press began to report on the same phenomena. To most it was a welcome development in an otherwise depressing scene. Journalists couldn't get over the happiness, sincerity and the integrity of sane, sensible, highly trained and often academic church leaders.

Much of what has marked the church in the 20th century in western Europe has not pleased God. It is inevitable that the recent phenomena may be used by some for their own ends. However, it is in marked contrast to the apathy on the one hand, and to ungodly practices on the other, that have infiltrated so many areas of church life. This is a breath of fresh air, bringing about the confession of sin, people drawing near to God and laughter, which in itself is therapeutic and helps us see things in a fresh perspective. It could be the prelude to something even more significant, perhaps the most significant thing that has hit the church for generations.

*

I was invited to the London Bible College, unofficially but with tutors' approval. I was to answer questions after an afternoon prayer meeting and there was to be an evening teaching meeting with a charismatic emphasis. Far more people came in the afternoon than expected. The evening meeting was so packed that it was overflowing to the hallway and stairs. After sensitive worship, I spoke for 20 minutes and the Holy Spirit then came upon the gathering in power. Chairs were hastily moved as the scene began to resemble a battlefield. There was the crying of repentance and the laughter of release.

Peter was one of those who came to the front for ministry. I prayed over him and had a word of prophecy: 'There's nothing that's been written that can't be put right.' Then he gasped and crumpled to the floor. For some time he couldn't get up. He had written a 10,000-word dissertation about the charismatic movement which was very negative. Weeks later, at a Pioneer refreshing meeting, he said of me, 'I had hated this little man.' He had come to the meeting at LBC in a highly sceptical mood.

'But, as the scripture was unfolded, I felt deeply challenged,' he said.

He was in tears as he told how he had apologised to me and had gone to his tutors to tell them that he would now have to rewrite the conclusions in his thesis.

*

At the DAWN conference in the spring of 1992 I had spoken to the Salvation Army officers who were there. During the talk the Lord gave me a prophecy which spoke of the breath of God sweeping through them. The Lord would humble them, anointing them with wisdom about when to be in and out of uniform. Doors would be open to them and they would touch even the royal family, as well as those on the streets.

As I poured out my heart in the prophecy which I felt the Lord was giving me, my mind was raising questions. I didn't agree with ranks and uniforms. Would the Salvation Army hierarchy be prepared to go in a different direction? Then I felt the Lord break in: 'Thank you for your opinions, but I don't need them.' I felt chastised. I didn't actually understand what was going on. Some officers were in tears. Some time afterwards I discovered that the prophecy had been transcribed and circulated to every Salvation Army citadel.

In July 1994 Michael Green and I were invited to the Salvation Army evangelists' conference. The prime mover in this was Phil Wall and there were 309 present. The Salvation Army had indeed been through a time of humbling, over the widely-publicised missing funds. It was the first time anything like this had happened. It had caused much heartache and had affected offerings. In the evening session, with the permission of Commander Dinsdale Pinder, I invited the senior officers forward, for Michael Green and me to anoint them with olive oil from Jerusalem. About 15 came forward. We anointed them on the forehead, offered prayer, and gave words of knowledge. Some were in tears.

No ministry was going on in the main body of the hall. People were just sitting. Suddenly, a man in the middle stood and started to give little jumps, knocking into others. Some fell to their knees, some raised their hands. Some shook, while others simply rested in the Spirit. Michael Green and I moved among them, praying with a few. Some collapsed, some laughed. We encouraged ministry one to another. Very few had experienced anything like this before. We should have finished at 9.30. By about 11.30 many people were prostrate. Sins were being confessed and deep gratitude was being expressed to the Lord.

I have met officers since who told me that they were so excited by what the Lord was doing that they never slept at all that night. Some who had been sceptical told me that the changes that had been wrought in lives led them to conclude that this could only be a work of the Spirit of God. It has been continuing in the lives of individual evangelists and in their corps. Many people have already been won for Christ.

*

It has been known that some tension existed between a Pentecostal denomination and Pioneer. This was partly because of the way a couple of churches and ministries had left to link up with Pioneer. The 'losers' felt a bit sore. Several meetings were held with the leaders to try to sort out differences. There were phone calls and correspondence.

Some progress had been made but several issues had still to be resolved. A meeting was arranged at a London hotel. When we all arrived, there were warm greetings and I noticed how light the atmosphere had become. We began telling stories and the other two leaders kept laughing.

Over breakfast we began to tease out the issues before us. But 'holy mirth' so overcame one of the leaders, a well-known figure in Christian circles, that he had to stuff a napkin in his mouth. Finally, in full view of other guests in the dining room, he tried to hide under the table. Later he was led of the Spirit to apologise for anything he had done to cause the rift between us.

I have since heard from him that this 'refreshing' has revolutionised their own executive meetings and relationships.

*

It was in one of our Sunday evening meetings, during a time of laughing, crying and resting in the Spirit. One of my leaders came to me. 'Please pray with me, I am in trouble,' he almost pleaded. Within a few moments I discovered he was under colossal sexual pressure, battling with temptation and the guilt of fantasy. On top of which he was endeavouring to keep a right attitude towards his wife, and was fighting off disappointment. There was no other physical sexual relationship involved and no videos or pornographic literature. 'But it is the presence of the Lord,' he explained, 'because of his presence, I can't live with this any longer.'

I prayed for him; he collapsed on the floor. He stayed there for perhaps 45 minutes. I had no need to speak to him again that evening. I phoned him the next morning. 'So what happened to you last night?' I enquired. 'I am not sure,' he replied. 'I felt I was in prison, and the door was about to slam shut on me. I knew I had to come to you for prayer. 'When you prayed for me, I consciously resisted the Holy Spirit. I decided I would not go down or collapse on the floor. Then it was like a magnet, drawing all my strength out of me. I collapsed.' He sobbed, 'I know, whatever was happening to me, Jesus was down there with me.'

Within a week of that encounter, one of our young evangelists spoke to me. 'What on earth has happened to John? He is completely different. At first I thought he had won a prize, but he has been like that all week now.' Sitting by the lake near my home, a week or two later, John commented, 'I am just completely different. I have the joy of the Lord in my heart and the fear of God on my soul.'

*

Mark is a young church leader on the south coast. I prayed for him at a leadership conference. He wept uncontrollably, collapsed into his chair and appeared semi-conscious. He was overcome by the presence of God. He led four people to Christ that week, and seven more within a week. Within a month 30 people either made a first-time response to Christ or he led them back into a relationship with Christ after they had gone away from God.

One woman, whose name needs to remain confidential, came to me recently. She had been taken in by a family 10 years ago and had been taken advantage of sexually.

She had discussed this with a friend, turned away from that sort of behaviour and to all intents and purposes it had been dealt with. But such was the presence of God in her church through manifestations, that she came to speak to me, as she was still living under a cloud of guilt. She explained the whole story, accepted responsibility for her part in what happened, found forgiveness in the eyes of God and acceptance among her peers. She told me a week or two later, 'I just feel completely different, and I am praying God's blessing on the man who took advantage of me.'

David was from a church in a nearby county. He was in a senior position in the church. He was prayed for, was clearly filled with the Spirit and touched by God in a fresh way, but there were no apparent outward strange manifestations. Afterwards I was told that it was one of the most significant experiences of his life. He had been terribly abused as a boy, physically, verbally and sexually. He had never, ever been able to laugh publicly since. That day as we prayed with him, he giggled and laughed and had a wide smile. A small thing to us, but so vitally important to him, his wife and his family and friends.

Jonathan had been through a tough time. He loved his job but was in tremendous financial difficulties, blaming others and perhaps unintentionally blaming God. In a letter to me he said it had been a most difficult two or three years. He was prayed with at one of our meetings, and was so filled with the Holy Spirit that he couldn't stand.

The experience has transformed him – and his wife too. He has gained dignity, respect and value.

16

A view from history

We can accept or reject what believers in former ages have said on a particular subject. But it can be helpful at least to see that what we face is not new. **Dr Ron Davies** considers physical manifestations, and reactions to them, in revival in the 18th century.

On the subject of strange and unusual physical manifestations in times of revival, the 18th-century theologian Jonathan Edwards gives a number of very useful insights. In the Great Awakening in New England, in which Edwards had a prominent place, there were all kinds of strange physical occurrences which different leaders reacted to in different ways.

Edwards mentions effects on the bodies of men: such as 'tears, trembling, groans, loud outcries, agonies of body, or the failing of bodily strength [also] persons fainting with joyful discoveries made to their souls . . . several instances of persons' flesh waxing cold and benumbed, and their hands clenched, yea, their bodies being set into convulsions.'

In one instance, probably that of his own wife Sarah, he describes

> very great effects on the body, nature often sinking under the weight of divine discoveries, the strength of the body taken away, so as to deprive of all ability to stand or speak; sometimes the hands clenched, and the flesh cold, but senses still remaining; animal

93

nature often in a great emotion and agitation, and the soul very often . . . so overcome with great admiration and a kind of omnipotent joy, as to cause the person (wholly unavoidably) to leap with all the might, with joy and mighty exultation of soul.

What did Edwards make of such things? His assessment can be best understood in contrast to what others were saying at the same time. Indeed, it is interesting to see a similar range of responses to the same phenomena today.

Charles Chauncy, a prominent Boston minister of the time, is a good example of those who wholeheartedly rejected the strange phenomena, and with them, the whole revival movement. He preached and wrote on the subject, his most prominent contribution being *Seasonable Thoughts on the State of Religion in New England* (1743). When George Whitefield and Gilbert Tennent were preaching to great crowds in Boston in 1740 and 1741, Chauncy kept quiet, but after they had gone he became more and more vocal in opposing the revival. He actually made a tour of New England collecting evidence of the excesses of various preachers and their hearers to include in his book.

He did his best to discredit the whole movement in a number of ways. He associated it with wild, heretical movements of the past which had exhibited similar phenomena. He described in lurid detail the worst excesses of the movement. He defined what to him was the essence of true religion, which was a religion of 'enlightened mind, not raised affections'. The revival, in his view, was no more than 'the effect of enthusiastic heat. . . and a commotion in the passions'.

Chauncy's response is in stark contrast with that of another prominent minister, who was in fact the target of much of Chauncy's attack, the Rev James Davenport of Long Island. Davenport started an itinerant ministry of his own in New England in 1741 and seems to have deliberately produced and encouraged the most bizarre and extreme kinds of physical reactions in his hearers.

The various reports which appeared in public newspapers about him probably exaggerated some of the things that happened in his meetings. But there is no doubt that he judged the presence of the Spirit by the degree of noise and eccentric behaviour and deliberately sought to encourage extremes of physical display. He eventually made a public apology for much of his behaviour but for many he brought the whole revival into disrepute.

The position of Jonathan Edwards may seem to be a calculated compromise between these two extreme stances. But it was his intention to make his own unique contribution. He discerned the essence of the revival experience and examined the reasons for such unusual phenomena accompanying the genuine work of the Spirit.

Four of his writings are given over to describing and analysing the two major revivals that took place in New England during his ministry, in both of which he was intimately involved.

They are all in the (more or less) complete two-volume edition of his works published by the Banner of Truth Trust, and three of them are also published separately by the same publisher. They are *A Faithful Narrative of the Surprising Work of God . . .* (1737), *The Distinguishing Marks of a Work of the Spirit of God* (1741), *Some Thoughts on the Revival in New England* (1742) and *A Treatise Concerning Religious Affections* (1746).

In *The Distinguishing Marks* he includes among nine factors which are 'no evidences that a work . . . is not the work of the Spirit of God' those 'effects on the bodies of men' mentioned above. His point is that such bodily effects are no evidence 'one way or the other'. The Scriptures are our only sure guide, and so

> We can't conclude that persons are under the influence of the true Spirit because we see such effects upon their bodies because this is not given as a true mark of the Spirit: nor on the other hand have we any reason to conclude from any such outward appearances that persons are not under the influence of the Spirit of God because there is no rule of Scripture given us to judge of spirits by that does

either expressly or indirectly exclude such effects on the body.

He goes on to say that it is quite understandable that an overwhelming personal awareness of divine realities should have effects of a physical kind, even of a dramatic and 'extraordinary kind; such as taking away the bodily strength, or throwing the body into great agonies, and extorting loud outcries'. But, on the other hand, such behaviour is no proof of the genuineness of such spiritual experience. There may be other factors at work, and probably are, according to Edwards.

The genuine work of the Holy Spirit is so often mixed with 'imprudences and irregularities' due to human weakness and fallenness, to undiscerned spiritual pride in those who experience these things, and to the work of Satan who both counterfeits the true work of God and also drives those who have genuinely known the Spirit's work into excesses.

What he has to say about the danger of spiritual pride and about the activity of Satan in connection with genuine revivals is of importance for assessing the work of renewal today. In *The Distinguishing Marks*, Edwards selects five characteristics of the revival, which in his view marked it as genuine:

- [ ] the fact that it exalted Jesus Christ;
- [ ] it attacked the kingdom of darkness;
- [ ] it honoured the Scriptures;
- [ ] it promoted sound doctrine;
- [ ] it resulted in an outpouring of love to God and man expressed in practical ways.

In *Some Thoughts*, and even more in *A Treatise Concerning Religious Affections*, he tries to separate true experiences of revival and conversion, even if they are accompanied by errors and irregularities, from those which are basically manifestations of self-love. The latter might still display high emotional states, extravagant spiritual talk and praise of God.

True experiences of the renewing work of the Holy Spirit are

God and Christ-centred, focusing on an adoring appreciation of the divine glory and grace, divorced from self-interest and self-glory, leading to humility, meekness, a spirit of forgiveness towards others, and a hungering and thirsting for righteousness. This is the antithesis of self-congratulation and a sense of having arrived. True experience of the grace of God will lead on to works of mercy and justice towards others, in personal concern for individuals and in social concern.

In Some Thoughts, he gives an account of one person whose experiences were highly ecstatic and quite remarkable. It is generally agreed that, although Edwards does not say so, he is describing his own wife's experience. In his view, hers is a good example of a number of the unusual physical phenomena manifest in the revival, but with a Christ-centredness and with practical outworkings which evidenced the experience as genuine. He describes the physical phenomena mentioned above, but in such a way as to emphasise that they are really only incidental to Sarah's spiritual experience.

Jonathan Edwards is aware that sceptics like Chauncy will dismiss all this as extreme irrational religious behaviour. His own, rather wry, comment is:

> If such things are enthusiasm and the fruits of a distempered brain, let my brain be evermore possessed of that happy distemper! If this be distraction, I pray God that the whole world of mankind may be seized with this benign, meek, beneficent, beatifical, glorious distraction!

He would encourage us similarly not to dismiss a movement out of hand because there are unusual and often inexplicable physical manifestations accompanying it. Nor, on the other hand, should we focus on or encourage the extreme and bizarre accompaniments.

Rather, we should emphasise and seek fellowship with the Lord, a closeness to him and the practical outworking in holiness and love.

17

Flow, river, flow

First the river is ankle deep, then knee deep, next it reaches the waist and soon becomes impossible to cross . . . The **Rev Mike Breen** sees an important message in Ezekiel for today's spiritual renewal.

I settled back into my chair and began thinking of the days ahead. St Louis to Gatwick, Gatwick to Sheffield and then home to the United States again.

'Cabin staff prepare the cabin for take-off, doors to automatic and cross-check' . . . we would soon be in the air and crossing the Atlantic. I was on my way to meet the leaders and preach at my new church in Sheffield. The morning congregations would hear a message from Revelation 2 which was specifically for them. The evening was more general: 'What is God doing Britain today and where are we in the process of spiritual renewal?' I felt sure that the answers were to be found in the book of Ezekiel.

Ezekiel 47 pictures a river flowing from within the temple in Jerusalem. From there it flows eastwards past a grove of fruit trees eventually descending into the Jordan rift valley, filling up the Dead Sea basin.

Night comes quickly when you are flying east. I knew that, as well as preparing, I would need to sleep before arriving in England. But my mind was so full of what the passage had to say that I wondered whether I would get any rest. As I looked at Ezekiel 47, it seemed that the vision of the river provided a pattern of renewal which had a beginning, a middle and an end.

It begins at the temple where a stream, hardly more than a trickle, begins to flow. The water flows over the threshold, past the altar and out of the south gate of Temple Mount. The stream then turns eastward and continues to flow. Renewal begins in God's presence, especially in worship. Sacrifice is unavoidable – the stream flows past the altar. In worship we are over-shadowed by the cross of Jesus and God calls us to lay down our lives in service and obedience to him.

The river continues to flow out of the south gate. In the days of Ezekiel, worshippers would always enter by the north gate and leave by the south, taking with them what they had received. So it is with the process of renewal. The direction is outwards.

As the river continues to flow from the south gate so it deepens. First the river is ankle deep, then knee deep, next it reaches the waist and soon becomes impossible to cross. To follow the renewing life of God's Spirit means getting into deeper and deeper water until our feet are off the bottom and he is fully in control.

It was at this point of surrendering control that Ezekiel was shown more. He was taken to the bank of the river where there were trees: their fruit continued throughout the year and their leaves were used for healing.

As the work of God's Spirit deepens we discover that meeting God in the temple of his presence and laying down our lives on the altar of obedience leads to the place where he is able to use us for the blessing and benefit of others. Our lives produce a continuous harvest of spiritual food and the wholeness and healing that God brings to us are shared with others.

Still the river, now a mighty torrent, continues to flow. At first the trickle becomes a stream, then the stream becomes a river, now the river unstoppable cascades towards its destination. The best anyone can do in a river like this is to stay afloat. The river is not only too deep and strong to cross, it is now too powerful to hope for anything but survival if you happen to be in it.

The river's destination is the Dead Sea, the lowest point on the face of the earth. To reach the Dead Sea, the river would leap and cascade down the newly formed cataracts and waterfalls that would punctuate the journey from the Judean uplands. Down the escarpment of the rift valley it would go, down to where Sodom and Gomorrah lay buried and where Lot's wife stands petrified for ever.

This place of death comes alive, teeming with fish and living creatures. There will be many places for spreading nets, harvesting the bounty of God's life-giving water. The life of God is flowing towards the deepest, deadest and most dismal parts of all creation. The purpose of renewal is to find the lost and bring life to those who have known only death. God's Spirit flows in to bring life and hope.

This process is very clear in Ezekiel 47 but does it represent a pattern for today? The answer is yes. Both in the Bible and in our own recent experience, we see a general pattern. Jesus followed this pattern. Luke 6.12–20 tells how he spent the night in the presence of his Father praying. After this he went with the twelve to the crowds of people who had gathered to listen. Healing poured forth from him, restoring many to wholeness and delivering others from the presence of evil spirits. Power was coming from him healing them all. He went on to share the good news with the spiritually dead and lost.

On a larger scale, we see Jesus in his baptism and temptation spending time with his Father, preparing for his mission. That mission was conducted for three years, feeding and healing both spiritually and physically the crowds that followed him. But the destination was the cross, resurrection and the commission to the twelve to preach the gospel to all the world, empowered by the Spirit who would come at Pentecost. This pattern can also be seen in the Acts of the Apostles.

Not wishing to over-simplify the process it is perhaps helpful to identify and name each of the three phases within this pattern of renewal.

Phase one: the temple. Encounter with God in worship and prayer. Laying aside ourselves and taking up the sacrifice of obedience.

Phase two: the trees. The call to give what we have received especially from the fruit of our lives and seeking healing and wholeness for those we meet.

Phase three: the terminus. Unconditional commitment to reaching the lost and seeing the spiritually dead brought to life.

Sitting on the plane thinking through this pattern, it struck me that my own experience was now midway through the process and I was waiting for the next stage. Like Ezekiel in his vision, I had followed the river of God and it was sweeping me along towards its goal.

I came into renewal through a fresh experience of God in worship. Like many in the 60s and 70s, I was excited to discover that the gifts were for today. The real presence of God working among his people in worship through the gifts of the Spirit was wonderful and tremendously exciting in the early days. Of course, it did not come without cost and often the sacrifices were very real. This was the temple. The altar. The gate. And the river flowing ever deeper towards the next stage.

As I stayed in the flow of what God was doing, I was able to maintain a modicum of control. But, in time the river carried me off my feet and I found myself in an orchard, or was it a Vineyard? The ministry of John Wimber, building on that of David Watson, brought to me the reality of God's sovereign power in the ministry of healing and casting out demons. What a fruitful time this was. We learned to pray for one another and many people were drawn to taste and see the goodness of God.

Where is the renewal going and what can we expect next? We can only expect that the river will become deeper and even more fast-flowing as it seeks its destination. We will eventually meet the 'Arabah' in which the Dead Sea is found. It is mentioned in Ezekiel 47 and literally means the 'great depression'. That's where the river is heading – where we least expect to find life. It is where people are gripped by death and judgment. That is where we will see a harvest. There will be many places for spreading nets.

Midway across the Atlantic I fell asleep and was awakened by the captain telling us that we were about to cross the coast of the British Isles. Since that week, when I came to share with St Thomas', I have moved back with my family from the States and have been inducted as the new team rector.

From the outset all that I have seen at St Thomas' and in other churches confirms to me we are in the beginning stages of a new phase of renewal. This is what we are seeing in the so-called 'Toronto wave'. The main elements of this wave may indicate where we are going. The joy may be the Lord strengthening his church for mission, 'for the joy of the Lord is our strength'.

The shaking may indicate that God is bringing forth his kingdom in us, shaking everything that can be shaken, so that what is unshakable – his kingdom – is revealed.

The refreshment may tell us that God is calling us to receive his life-giving water and give it to those who live in a spiritual desert.

If all of this is true, how should we continue to prepare? Of course, discernment needs to be exercised. But, if God is on the move, we must stay in the centre of the flow, at the heart of what God is doing among his people.

The best preparation for what God is going to do next is receiving what God is doing now. At St Thomas' we are earnestly seeking all that the Lord has for us, focusing on the fruit and not on the phenomena of the Spirit's presence. We are asking for a growth in holiness, while the Spirit of holiness, the Holy Spirit, is so powerfully present. We are looking to God to reveal his priorities, his agenda and are casting aside all else.

Anything that we are trying to take with us that is not suitable for the journey will be destroyed in the rapids and the waterfalls. When people shoot the rapids on the Colorado they go in large flexible rubber rafts. A cabin-cruiser or an ocean-going yacht would be smashed to pieces. We need to develop programmes and structures that are flexible enough to ride the currents but strong enough to hold us together.

Lastly, we need to heed the cautionary note God gives us in Ezekiel 47. He warns us that the swamps and marshes will not become fresh, they will be left for salt. Marshes and swamps occur when water is diverted onto a flat area of land and ceases to flow. Marshes often maintain a good deal of life; swamps are progressively more stagnant and support fewer and fewer life forms.

We need to ensure, as we receive the new life of the Spirit, that we do not divert that life for our own purposes. The living water of God's Spirit that is diverted for self-centred, self-seeking purposes will first become a marsh and then a swamp. These will be left for salt. In other words, they will be left for spiritual death and a final reckoning with God.

The charismatic movement has at times left the marsh and swamp of traditionalism or religion, only to divert the new life of the Spirit into a marsh or a swamp of its own making. We must follow the Spirit and not divert his life for our own purposes. We must follow the river wherever it leads as it accelerates, grows and deepens towards its destination.

What a destination that will be: revival in our land and the wholesale conversion of thousands of its people. May this come quickly!

18

Three R's from the Holy Spirit

A concluding chapter by **Wallace Boulton**, editor of *Renewal*.

Isaiah 55 begins with that wonderful invitation, 'Come, all you who are thirsty, come to the waters.' It is an invitation to everyone: young and old, well-off and deprived. The Lord excludes only those who exclude themselves. There is only one qualification needed: to be thirsty. Those who are self-satisfied don't thirst. They have no sense of need.

Physical thirst can lead to physical death. There can be desperation in the desert without water. There can be the mirage in the distance: what appears to be an oasis, but it is an illusion. There is a spiritual parallel. Without Christ, the living water, the human soul is dying. It is becoming parched and shrivelled, though physically a person may appear healthy. There is this gracious invitation, a longing on the part of God, that everyone who thirsts should come to the living water. 'This water that I shall give,' Jesus told the woman at the well, 'will become a spring of water, welling up to eternal life' (John 4.14).

It is the Holy Spirit who convicts a person of this need at the very heart of our being. There are many in our churches, however, who have come to personal faith at some point in their lives, who do know Jesus as their Lord and Saviour, and yet who have become parched. Church attendance has become routine, prayer seems without any real depth or meaning, the

Bible has become largely a closed book, the joy and vitality of being a Christian have gone.

The first of these three R's of the Holy Spirit is 'refreshing.' God promises to pour water on him who is thirsty and streams on the dry ground (Isaiah 44.3). The Lord longs to refresh his people and his Spirit is bringing that refreshing. There are showers of blessing on ground that has become very dry, on dry churches and dry Christians, so that once more may flow rivers of living water. In John 7.37–38 we read how Jesus proclaimed, 'If a man is thirsty, let him come to me and drink. Whoever believes in me, streams of living water will flow from within him' (NIV). In the following verse we read: 'Now this he said about the Spirit, whom those who believed in him were later to receive.'

The Holy Spirit comes to refresh the Lord's people. He is doing that today.

In the little town of Nazareth it is the Sabbath. Who is reading the lesson in the synagogue service? A young man steps forward. Jesus is reading the lesson. He opens the scroll and he reads verses from Isaiah. Then he rolls up the scroll and hands it back to the attendant. All eyes are upon him. He declares, 'Today this Scripture is fulfilled in your hearing.' Jesus has just outlined his calling or, as we might say today, his job description. But he has not been appointed, he has been anointed. To do what?

> To preach good news to the poor,
> to proclaim release to the captives and recovery of sight to the blind,
> to set at liberty those who are oppressed,
> to proclaim the acceptable year of the Lord. (Luke 4.18–19, RSV)

Who are the captives around us today? Who are the oppressed? There are many, many people in our communities who are hurting. Family life for many is under great strain and pressure, if not broken. Young lives have been marred. People are oppressed by sin. They are turning to other wells and are finding them dry. I looked at the faces in a long queue of people waiting to buy tickets in the national lottery. They looked drained and expressionless. These were people just hoping that this might give them a chance of release, of fulfilment, in their lives. The Lord longs to bring real release and real fulfilment into lives. He wants to set people really free, whatever the circumstances of life might still be.

There are Christians who still need to be set free. We may be people of faith, who have opened our heart to the Lord, and yet not be completely free. There may be guilt, or fears, or hurts being nursed. There may be some part of life from which the Lord is excluded, some little room which is still locked to him.

God the Holy Spirit is at work in our midst today. He is coming in power upon churches and individuals and he is bringing the second of the three R's—release. The Holy Spirit is coming upon men and women, and children too, that Jesus will be glorified in their lives. People are being released from their guilt, they are being cleansed and forgiven. People are being freed from their hurts and their fears.

When that happens, by the Spirit's power coming upon them, they are overwhelmed. They may fall to their knees, or lie on the ground, gently 'resting' in the Spirit, perhaps for a long period. They may cry out in repentance, they may laugh with the joy of release, they may express the intensity of the experience in other ways. This is a deeply personal experience, yet is no way embarrassing to them or to the people around them. Not everyone is affected in this way, indeed most people have not been on the occasions when I have witnessed this happening. Others have testified, however, to a deep sense of the Lord's presence and to personal anointing.

It must be added, about the manifestations we are seeing in this time of refreshing and release, that we do need discernment. There can also be manifestations which are of the flesh. Whenever God is at work, the enemy is going to be active, to try to disrupt and produce what is counterfeit.

Christian leaders have to be very discerning, to know what is truly the work of the Spirit and to encourage it, that the Spirit will have free reign, but at the same time to distinguish what is alien. The test is that, if the Holy Spirit is at work in a life, Jesus will be glorified. That life will reflect his glory. The released life is going to be a more fruitful life for him. That will be shown over a period of time, however; the leader may have to make an instant decision in a meeting about whether a particular manifestation is genuinely of the Spirit or not. Any person disrupting the work of the Spirit must be led out to another room.

The leader has an important responsibility in another respect. He or she must always remember that the Spirit is sovereign. We may be anxious to see the Holy Spirit working but we must resist the temptation to try to manipulate the meeting, or indeed the Spirit, to try to achieve what we are longing to see. A meeting should not be 'pumped up' before asking to God to send his Spirit. There must be great sensitivity to what he himself is wanting to do and how he is wanting to do it. Meetings have been almost spoilt for me by raucous singing, over and over again, of songs which should be sung quietly and prayerfully, or by requests made by the leader. At one meeting all the clergy present were asked to shout three times, 'I let go!' On every occasion, however, the Holy Spirit has nevertheless graciously come upon the meeting and lives have been powerfully touched and changed.

The third 'R' from the Holy Spirit is 'revival'. Those closely involved in the present movement of the Spirit have been rightly careful not to describe it as 'revival', though there is the feeling that we could be at the threshold of revival. Yes, we are seeing refreshing and release within the church, but we are not yet seeing revival. These may be signs that it is near, that the Lord is preparing his people. There is a great longing among Christians for revival, echoing Isaiah's words, 'Oh, that you would rend the heavens and come down' (Isaiah 64.1).

We do need to be clear about what revival is. Arthur Wallis, in his classic book on revival, *In the Day of Thy Power*, first published 39 years ago, gives this definition: 'Revival is God revealing himself in awful holiness and irresistible power. . . .It is such a manifest working of God that human personalities are overshadowed and human programmes abandoned.' A revival cannot be planned or organised. Indeed, the Holy Spirit can be 'organised out' of our churches. He is too unpredictable and too disturbing. There can be, however, and there must be, preparation, for revival. As Campbell Morgan put it: 'We can't organise revival, but we can set our sails to catch the wind when God chooses to blow on his people again.' Revival has often come when church life has been at a low ebb and when, socially and morally, a nation has been in a perilous state. England in the 18th century was in such a condition, before what has been termed 'the great awakening'. Christians in this country today may often feel despairing, but it is when we come to the end of our own resources, our own initiatives, our own self-confidence, and cast ourselves entirely upon God that we are at the first stage of preparation for revival.

The verse perhaps most often quoted in this connection is 2 Chronicles 7.14: 'If my people, who are called by my name, shall humble themselves and pray, and seek my face, and turn from their wicked ways, then will I hear from heaven, and will forgive their sin, and will heal their land.' There are several key thoughts about revival in this one verse. It is addressed to 'my people'. Something has to happen to the believers before it is going to happen among all the unbelievers. There is 'humbling' and prayer involved in preparation for revival. Above all, there is the need for repentance and forgiveness. Every recorded revival has been preceded by prayer: persevering, sacrificial prayer. When revival came, it was marked by an overwhelming sense of the power and holiness of God. In the face of this, individuals were overcome with the sense of their own sin and utter unworthiness. It was an intolerable burden. Hardened Welsh miners broke down in the revival of 1904, weeping and pleading for God's mercy. It was God's forgiveness through

Christ, the lifting of this burden and the great sense of release, that led to the ecstacy and lasting joy which has marked every great revival.

An emphasis on repentance has been largely lost in today's church, a church that is often superficial and compromised. Cleansing and purifying within the church are, however, initial marks of revival. This note of repentance has been there in the experiences reported from churches touched by the present movement of the Holy Spirit, but it has not been the dominant theme. Perhaps it will be, as, please God, the movement of the Holy Spirit spreads byond the church.

Arthur Wallis wrote:

> This overwhelming sense of God, bringing deep conviction of sin, is perhaps the outstanding feature of true revival. The manifestation of it is not always the same. Sometimes it is predominantly the unconverted who are convicted. At other times it is Christians or professing Christians. . . .In times preceding revival it is common to find among believers of various persuasions a fresh emphasis on the person and work of the Holy Spirit. Many have been lost in a maze of theological controversy. Others have moved for years in a rut of traditional interpretation, concerned with an explanation rather than an experience, a definition instead of a dynamic.
>
> (*In the Day of Thy Power*, Christian Literature Crusade, 1956)

Another mark of every great revival has been its effect on the whole community. It is too early in the present movement of the Spirit to expect to see this distinctive feature. If, however, we do not begin to see it, we will not be entering into revival.

In the Ulster revival of 1859, crime fell so dramatically that magistrates found themselves with nothing to do. One report of the Welsh revival of 1904 states that nothing had ever come over Wales with such far-reaching results. 'Confessions of awful sins were heard on every side. Old debts were paid. The pit ponies refused to work, being unused to kindness. In five weeks, 20,000 people joined the churches.'

Sadly, however, within a few years that great revival petered out. We know from the New Testament that the Holy Spirit can be grieved and can be quenched. Revivals have ended through division, through excesses, through compromise, through reverting to human methods.

Revival is the greatest need of the church and the nation. Let us be ready. Let us be fit vessels and be open to whatever the Holy Spirit would do in us and through us.

Come, Holy Spirit, in the fullness of your power, that Jesus may be honoured and glorified among us.

Appendix I

Guidelines for leaders

What should leaders do when the Holy Spirit comes? These guidelines were prepared by **Gerald Coates**, with help from **Bryn Jones**, **Sandy Millar**, **David Pytches** and Vineyard USA.

1 Make a swift response to the work of the Spirit

We must be willing to embrace the work of God's Spirit even if it means changes to our structures, programmes and agendas. The main key is the entire leadership submitting themselves to the Holy Spirit and being willing to receive prayer.

2 Respond with humility and faith

Faith will overcome our fears, uncertainty and doubt. Humility will keep us from superiority and elitism. We have been praying for renewal and revival, we should not be surprised if God responds. 'Which of you if his son asked for bread would give him a stone? Or if he asked for a fish would give him a snake?' (Mt 7.9,10)

3 Take responsibility for what is happening

The elders in Corinth had a hands-off approach. It was a mixture of manifestations of the Spirit, the work of the flesh and even the devil. As leaders we have to give an account for what we allow and encourage in our churches.

4 Ensure that we are overseeing and administering what is going on

We do not want things simply to become introspective. We want to see people ultimately look to those outside the Christian community. Otherwise self indulgence will take root, and either we will be responding to people's needs and manifestations or, eventually, we will dry up.

Practical help

Ensure that you do not seek personal gain, prominence or benefit from what is clearly a divine visitation.

Do not develop a ministry of manifestations, when God is wanting to do something deeper.

Do not hype meetings, be relaxed but full of expectancy.

Maintain a focus on the source of the blessing, Christ himself and do not transfer people's faith either to a person, a place or a method.

Do not be afraid of praying with children as well as adults. Most children believe this to be a little like heaven and are much more responsive than some adults. When praying with children it is helpful to have parents or a parent present. If parents have been touched by God we should be looking out for their children.

Explain any unusual activities. It may be of God or the devil but you will be responsible for determining which. Do not leave the church confused.

Endeavour to understand that events like these place great demands on you as a leader emotionally and physical. Ensure you rest; do not stagger from meeting to meeting.

Enjoy what is going on, do not become over heavy, serious and certainly not religious.

Be prepared for criticism. Some will not understand what is going on, others will be fearful. This is a time for sensitive action not emotional reaction.

While not discouraging people from visiting other churches to see what is happening, be wary of competitiveness and comparisons. Also, of people simply running around to 'get blessed' without that blessing being allowed to bring about a radical change of life.

Be careful about prolonged times of men praying for women or women men. It is preferable that prayer should be single-sex or in groups.

If there is a fleshly or demonic manifestation which you are unable to deal with make sure someone is drawn alongside you immediately. Such manifestations can be a distraction to the rest of the meeting.

Encourage people when they feel that 'nothing has happened'. Some have sat under this sort of ministry for up to 12 hours with 'nothing happening' but now they are prominent channels of this blessing.

Facing opposition

There has never been a move of God which has not faced serious opposition. We see this in Jesus' ministry and in the Acts of the Apostles from the religious as well as the godless.

So we need to minister to the Lord and his people with 'clean hands and a pure heart'. Therefore let us ensure that our behaviour is in line with the biblical mandate, with as little physical contact as possible, never pushing people over, or saying things which amount to triumphalism or pure fantasy. Don't invite criticism and opposition.

When we are attacked by people in the church, or other churches, or in the Christian press, it is easy to be reactionary, cynical, dismissive or superior. This could be more a matter of attitude than word, and comes across with a 'What do they know?' attitude. Remain calm, rational and reasonable. Learn to disagree without being disagreeable.

Endeavour to read Scripture into what is going on, without becoming preachy or sermonising. We must not be awash in a sea of subjectivity.

Create a worshipping environment and give room for testimonies that speak of the fruit rather than the manifestations.

Encourage people to 'drink' as Jesus promises to quench our thirst. Also encourage people to allow the rivers of living water to touch those outside the Christian community.

Wait on God. Things cannot be rushed. Jesus told the early disciples to wait with expectancy in the upper room. It took days not moments.

Encourage a continual response. C H Spurgeon, when asked why he needed to be continually filled with the Spirit, responded 'Because I leak!' We should not be surprised when people keep responding; they are thirsty and needy.

Encourage people to release their emotions. We are still a very controlled people. We are suspicious of anything emotional. Laughter, tears, shouting, or physical jerks must be allowed to happen.

Ensure that those leading meetings, or who are praying with others, share the vision of the church, support the leadership and are open to the activity of the Holy Spirit.

Do not become so taken up with the meeting that you fail to oversee the event. Ensure that you have a group of trusted, senior people who can minister to those responding.

When you pray for people
When people's strength fails them, keep praying for them. Encourage them to stay down where they are and receive from the Lord. It is not unusual for people to stay down on the floor for significant periods.

Do not be afraid of having people catching those falling down. It removes the unnecessary fear of falling, bumps or collision and while it is not vital it is helpful.

Create floor space even if it means moving chairs. We are responsible for facilitating the work of the Holy Spirit.

Do not in any way manipulate the activity of the Holy Spirit. People must not be allowed to believe this is the work of human beings, but the work of God.

Encourage people to remain open to God: not looking for manifestations but a work of the Spirit seen or unseen.

*

The Pioneer People leadership team was recently given a vision of a heart, where the input valves were fine but the output valves were fractured. Barbed wire was also seen around the heart. To one side was a workman's bench and tools with nails.

I believe the interpretation was for our leadership team and may be appropriate for you. The heart is the heart of the church, which is the key leader, the leadership team and the committed members.

God is 'inputting', but when we get criticised, or there is a reactionary note to what is going on, we can react, get angry and generally marginalise those who do not understand what is going on or how are fearful.

The barbed wire speaks of defensiveness. Reacting can distract us from the work bench, where we are being asked to build rather than knock down, to put together rather than marginalise.

We must be prepared for opposition. We should expect it and count it all joy when we go through it and simply be willing to pray for people and bless them, treating them with courtesy.

Continually giving out, without receiving, can lead to exhaustion and burn-out. Take time to receive, rest, read Scripture and do 'normal' things. God wants us around for the long haul not a short sprint.

APPENDIX 2

Leading others into the baptism of the Holy Spitit

'Have you been baptised in the Holy Spirit?' the counsellor asked **Peter Gammons**. 'I've never heard of it,' he replied. 'But if I need it, I'll have it.' He describes how the prayer that followed started a whole new dimension of Christian living for him.

Over the years I have noticed how similar my own experience was to that of many of those I counselled. I was truly born again. I had experienced a powerful encounter with the Lord and could even remember the day and hour when it happened. However, I knew that there was something missing in my life. The more I read the Book of Acts, the more I saw how powerless my own Christian life was.

I had tried to witness, but my words just seemed to bounce back without effect. I also felt guilty, as Bible study and prayer were not as alive as I knew that they should be.

I went to the meeting mentioned in the introduction, having already decided to go forward for prayer. I found that the baptism in the Spirit was the key to each of my dilemmas.

Jesus had said that the Holy Spirit would teach (Jn 14.26), guide (Jn 16.13) and empower the believer (Ac 1.8). Concerning God's Word, Jesus had said, 'When the Spirit of truth is come, he will lead you into all truth.' God's Word is 'the sword of the Spirit' (Eph 6.17). As the author of God's Word, the Holy Spirit can enlighten it for us. From that day God's

Word came alive to me in a new way, as if it were written in three dimensions.

Concerning witnessing, Jesus said, 'You shall receive power when the Holy Spirit comes upon you and you shall be witnesses for me. . .' (Ac 1.8). Within three days of receiving the empowering of the Holy Spirit, I led my first soul to Christ. Within three days they had led someone to Christ. So, within six days I was a 'spiritual grandad'!

For some readers, it may have been so long ago that you were baptised in the Holy Spirit, that you have almost forgotten the amazing difference that this empowering made. However, I have found that this empowering has been the solution to many of the problems in Christian lives. I believe that second only to knowing how to lead a person to Christ, must be knowing how to lead someone into the baptism in the Spirit.

The baptism in the Holy Spirit released me into a whole new dimension of prayer (Rm 8.26). Above all, this Holy Spirit empowering made Jesus so much more real, for Jesus said that the Holy Spirit would glorify him.

I was baptised in the Spirit during the early days of the charismatic renewal in Britain. At the time, some were saying, 'All this teaching on the baptism in the Spirit is of the devil.' I remember one preacher saying, 'If this baptism in the Spirit is of the devil, then the devil must have got converted, because it glorifies Jesus.'

Let me share with you then eight helpful steps in leading others into the baptism in the Spirit.

1 Point them to Jesus

He is the baptiser in the Holy Spirit (Mt 3.11).

2 Explain the importance of the baptism in the Spirit

Jesus attributed the miracles and powerful results of his ministry to the anointing of the Holy Spirit (Lk 4.18) and promised his followers this same empowering (Jn 14.16,26; Ac 1.8).

Jesus told his disciples to wait in Jerusalem until they had received this baptism in the Spirit. He warned them that, even after three years of having walked as his close companions, they could not be the effective witnesses that he had called them to be without this empowering (Lk 24.49). If Jesus needed the empowering of the Holy Spirit (Mt 3.16), how much more do we?

3 Don't get hung up on terminology

The Scriptures differentiate between baptism by the Spirit into the body of Christ at conversion (1 Cor 12.13) and Christ baptising the believer in the Holy Spirit (Jn 1. 33). Hebrews 6.2 speaks of 'the doctrine of baptisms' (plural). We miss out if we confuse them.

Nevertheless, we must not major on what we call this experience. For example, in Acts 1.4–5, Jesus said that his followers would be 'baptised in the Holy Spirit' and Acts 2.4 tells us that they were 'filled with the Spirit'. It does not matter what you call it, just get it!

4 Encourage them to receive by faith

This empowering is available for every believer. Salvation is God's free gift to the sinner; the baptism in the Spirit is God's free gift to the saints. Concerning the Holy Spirit, Jesus promised that everyone who asked would receive (Lk 11.13). Therefore, we can ask in faith expecting to receive (Gal 3.14).

5 Speaking in tongues was the most common manifestation in the Bible that a person had received

It is good to explain this before you pray together. See Acts 2. 4; 10.45-46; 19.2–6. There has been so much negative teaching on this subject, that it may hinder the person from fully receiving unless you explain it clearly from God's Word.

I am not seeking to emphasise tongues above the other gifts. However, this gift is different, in that the other gifts are primarily for ministering to others; tongues is for ministering to the Lord and for edifying ourselves spiritually (1 Cor 14.2, 4). When a person asks, 'Do I have to speak in tongues?' it shows that they do not understand the purpose of this precious gift. If they did, they would ask, 'May I please have this gift.'

When I pray in English, I can only pray for those things which I know about. But, when I pray in tongues, the Holy Spirit can tune me in to pray for those things that I do not know about. He can tune me in to intercede during emergencies or even to pray for deep needs in my own life that I could not express in my own words. God may have even been tuning me in to pray for you for months. This precious gift opens up a new dimension of miracle living.

Who is the Holy Spirit? God. Who do I pray to? God. Does God know what the will of God is? Of course!

When a person prays in tongues they are praying perfect prayers. Can you see why the devil seeks to denigrate this gift?

6 Explain that to use this or any other gift a person must take a step of faith

You may need to explain that God will use their tongue and lips to form the words and to speak them out.

Some modern translations of the Scriptures talk of 'ecstatic tongues'. I can only assume that this is because the translator did not understand this gift, for the word 'ecstatic' is not in the original Greek text. God is not a ventriloquist. Paul said, 'I will pray in the Spirit and I will pray with the understanding.' It was an act of his will.

Some people have said, 'I just began to speak in a new language. I could not help it.' That kind of testimony can be misleading. I understand what they mean. But theologically I disagree; they could have helped it. The truth is, because they were surrendered to Christ, the gift of tongues just flowed.

God does not possess people, he co-operates. We read of the 120 on the day of Pentecost, 'They began to speak in other tongues as the Spirit gave them utterance.' Notice that they did the speaking, but the Holy Spirit gave them the words. The miracle is not in the speaking, but in the content of what the Holy Spirit causes us to say.

Encourage them to begin to speak out new words, trusting God that they will be the right ones. Some people keep praying, 'O Lord, give me the gift of tongues. O Lord, give me the gift of tongues.' There comes a time when they have to stop speaking in English and switch into overdrive! You cannot speak in two languages at the same time.

Some people are waiting for the Holy Spirit to do something, while he is waiting for them to do something – to take a step of faith.

7 Pray for them expecting them to receive

Finally, having shared these points to deal with any of their doubts and questions, pray for them expecting them to receive.

Encourage those you are seeking to help to pray, 'Thank you, Lord, that you have poured out your Holy Spirit. Thank you that you promised that if I asked, I would receive. Lord, I now receive the empowering of your Holy Spirit in Jesus' name. Thank you, Lord, that you are faithful to your promises. Amen.'

8 Remind them that the baptism in the Spirit is for a purpose

Every blessing that we receive is so that we might be a blessing to others. God said to Abraham, 'I will bless you and through you all the nations of the earth shall be blessed.' When the early church received the baptism in the Spirit, they were driven out onto the streets and 3,000 people were converted that day.

Jesus said, 'Out of your innermost being shall flow rivers of living water.' He wants you to be blessed, but he also wants others to be touched by the overflow. When those rivers of living waters truly flow, if others get near, they will get wet!

Jesus said, 'You shall receive power when the Holy Spirit is come upon you and you will be witnesses to me. . . .' The ultimate purpose of Pentecost is to make us living witnesses for Jesus. God has not poured out his Holy Spirit so that we can just enjoy 'bless-me-up' meetings. As someone once put it, 'If you don't use the blessing, you will lose the blessing.'

This was one of the major mistakes many made in the early

days of the charismatic movement. We 'got blessed' but we didn't take that blessing out to the world. God is pouring out his Spirit afresh on the church at this time, to anoint us to finish the great task Jesus set us, to complete the Great Commission.

Let us not fail our Lord, but go, in the power of the Holy Spirit and take the gospel to every creature.

APPENDIX 3

An evangelical consultation

A group of evangelical leaders met in December 1994 at the invitation of the Evangelical Alliance to discuss their various opinions on the Toronto blessing. The following statement was issued in mid-January:

In relation to what has come to be known as the Toronto blessing, a consultation of some leading evangelicals recognised the need not only to evaluate such experiences but also to make clear distinctions between primary and secondary convictions among us. We therefore reaffirm the overwhelming measure of agreement among us as evangelicals, even though we differ in our initial interpretations of these experiences.

1 We affirm together the classic evangelical convictions. The Scriptures are the inspired Word of God; our faith is centred on the person and atoning work of Christ; we stress the vital need for personal conversion; we are committed to active witness and service in the world.

2 We affirm the centrality of the Great Commission to the task of the church. We also rejoice that in our history God has poured out his Spirit in revivals, and these are intrinsic to the evangelical heritage we share.

3 We affirm the indivisible unity of the Word and Spirit. The

Scriptures are God-breathed and their authority cannot be diminished. The Holy Spirit who inspired the unchanging Scriptures applies them to our lives, to both our minds and our hearts. We seek to live under the authority of the Word and in the power of the Spirit. The essence of work of the Spirit according to the Scriptures includes the following:

Christ is central and glorified.

Hunger grows for the Word and for prayer.

Awareness of the holiness of God leads to repentance and holiness of life.

Spiritual gifts are distributed and exercised in the church.

Preaching becomes empowered.

The love and joy of god are poured into our hearts.

Greater passion arises for the lost, without God and without hope.

Greater compassion arises for the disadvantaged, demonstrated in social action.

Where the Spirit's work is intensified, we would expect to see a heightened awareness of these distinctives.

4 The Spirit of God comes to clothe the church with power from on high, both in the ongoing processes of continuing church life and growth, and also in dramatic periods of revival.

5 Where we differ, we remain committed to evangelical unity, based on our common convictions and priorities under the Lordship of Christ. We confess that in the past this unity has sometimes been undermined by a failure to listen to one another, and by a readiness to caricature and denigrate those with whom we disagree. In this consultation we have sought to ask questions of ourselves and one another, without compromising the integrity of our conscientiously held differences.

6 Where there have been revivals, there has generally been an increase in the frequency of manifestations associated with repentance and conversion and also with the joy of new abundant life in Christ. However, we are clear that these

manifestations are secondary. Physical and emotional manifestations cannot in themselves prove that a movement is or is not a work of God. The test is the lasting, biblical fruit. No one should seek manifestations as an end in themselves. Rather, we need to seek to grow in the knowledge of God and in his service.

7   At present we are inevitably seeing that experience is not yet integrated with theological reflection. We rejoice with those who have known genuine life-changing encounters with the holiness and majesty, power and love of the risen Christ. We reject any tendency to pursue manifestations as an end in themselves. We regret that some have neglected the discipline of biblical preaching in the face of current manifestations, but we rejoice with those who speak of a new empowering in preaching in recent months. Our common priority is the proclamation of the gospel on fire.

8 We recognise that historical, theological and cultural influences can unconsciously condition our Christian perspective. The existentialist spirit of our age emphasises subjective experience and feelings over convictions and objective truth. We also recognise the equal and opposite danger of enlightenment rationalism, which has in the past resulted in dead orthodoxy which leaves no room for the direct intervention of the Spirit of God. We must guard and proclaim the absolute truth of the gospel without compromise.

9 We do not believe that the church in the United Kingdom is presently experiencing revival. However, many have testified to an increased sense of manifest presence of God in recent months, and to empowered preaching and conversions. This enrichment has been observed in some measure across the evangelical spectrum. This encourages us to hope that we may be in a period of preparation for revival.

10 The evaluation of present phenomena can only be provisional: it is too early for definitive judgments. While no

work of God takes place without a fleshly dimension, or even the possibility of demonic counterfeit, opinions differ markedly among evangelicals at present over precisely what is happening.

Some have grave reservations about the value and significance of recent events in many churches; others speak of 1994 as a year of remarkable spiritual refreshing. We therefore recognise the need for a group within the Evangelical Alliance to continue to provide evaluation and theological reflection on these developments in the church. We suggest that such a group should plan to review these questions in a year's time.

11 We readily endorse the classic tests of a genuine work of God, as expounded by Jonathan Edwards:

☐ Does it raise people's estimation of Jesus Christ?
☐ Does it operate against the interests of Satan?
☐ Does it lead to a greater regard for Scripture and truth?
☐ Does it result in a greater awareness of and seriousness about the things of God?
☐ Does it lead to a greater love for God, for other Christians and for the wider world?

12 Our nations, and indeed our continent and world, are in desperate need of the gospel. We therefore commit ourselves afresh to obey the command to proclaim the good news and make disciples, and call the church to pray for the outpouring of the spirit of God in revival power upon our land.

Graham Kins, David Cole, Alan Gibson, Gerald Coates, John Butcher, Robert Amess, Tony Baker, Rob Warner, Philip Mohabir, Faith Forster, Paul Perkin, Matthew Ashimolowo, Derek Tidball, Stephen Sizer, Clive Calver, Joel Edwards, Bryn Jones, Phil Hill, Philip Hacking, David Abernethie, Tudur Jones, R T Kendall, David Enoch

RENEWAL

THE PEOPLE, THE EVENTS,
THE GOD WHO ACTS

SPECIAL OFFER
to readers of
The Impact of Toronto

If you have enjoyed this book why not take out a subscription to
Renewal. Read each month about how the
Holy Spirit is at work today.

If you use the form opposite, you will qualify for the SPECIAL
OFFER of 13 issues for the price of 12, and our guarantee that
you can return your first magazine within 28 days for a full
refund if you are not completely satisfied.

ORDER FORM

(Please return to *Renewal* Subscriptions, Monarch
Magazines, FREEPOST TN1636, Broadway House,
The Broadway, Crowborough, East Sussex TN6 1BR;
no stamp needed.)

Please send me *Renewal* magazine for the next THIRTEEN
months FOR THE PRICE OF TWELVE.

I enclose a cheque/PO made payable to 'Renewal' for

☐   £22.00 (UK)
☐   £25.00 (Europe including Eire)
☐   £27.00 (Rest of World)

Please debit my credit card
by £_____: Mastercard/Visa
(Please delete as necessary)

☐ ☐ ☐ ☐ ☐ ☐ ☐ ☐ ☐ ☐ ☐ ☐ ☐ ☐ ☐ ☐

Credit card expiry date: ☐ ☐ / ☐ ☐

Signature ....

(BLOCK CAPITALS)
Name & Initials only (Rev)...
Rev/Dr/Mr/Mrs/Miss/Ms ....
Address ....
....
....
Postcode ....